God's Promises to You

BY REGIS CASTRO

Raïssa – 2nd edition
A way of Crome Life
Pique
Barby
Rabboni – 2nd edition
The Endearing Hands of Mary – 2nd edition
Book of Divine Mercy – 2nd edition
Cod's Advice for You – 3rd edition

BY REGIS CASTRO AND MAÏSA CASTRO

Jesus Loves You – 3rd edition
Jesus Visits You (Rachel) – 2nd edition
Healing through Blessing (Blessing upon Blessing) – 2nd edition
Jesus Is My Friend – 2nd edition
The Powerful Hand of Jesus in My Heart – 2nd edition
Jesus Wants to Heal Your Life – 3rd edition
Book of the Family – Healing and Salvation for You and Your Family – 2nd edition
Ping-Pong Praise – 2nd edition
Rosary of Liberation – 6th edition
Testimonials about the Rosary of Liberation
Eternal Love – 3rd edition

BY MAÏSA CASTRO

You Must Be Born Again
Persevere in the Love of God – 3rd edition
God's Promises to You
Prayers of Power – 3rd edition
Prayers of Power II
Pray for Us, O Holy Mother of God!

Maïsa Castro, ed.

GOD'S PROMISES TO YOU

Editors: Regis Castro/Maïsa Castro
Translation: Robert Hausemann
Revision: Vilma Ap. Albino/Gilbert R. Avellar
Cover: Estúdio Campos
Printed by: R. Vieira Gráfica e Editora Ltda./Campinas/SP

FOR THE GLORY OF JESUS CHRIST OUR LORD. ALLELUIA!

The biblical citations were taken from *The Jerusalem Bible*. Garden City, Doubleday & Company, Inc., 1968.

ISBN 85-7345-026-6 (original edition)
ISBN 85-7345-098-3

Orders from:

• **RABONI EDITORA LTDA**.
  C. P. 1700 – CEP 13001-970 – Campinas/SP – Brasil
  PHONE NUMBER: 0055-19-3242-8433
  FAX: 0055-19-3242-8505

  Home page: http://www.raboni.com.br
  e-mail: raboni@raboni.com.br

I dedicate this book to my father, Luiz Américo Lettiére, who encouraged me so much to write it and hoped to be able to see it published before going to his celestial home.

To all the sons and daughters of God, so that they may learn how to come into, through faith in Jesus Christ and in His Word, the possession of the greatest and most precious promise, and, consequently, become participants in the divine nature through them.

"Jesus Christ is the same today as he was yesterday and as he will be for ever"
(He. 13:8).

"However many the promises God made, the Yes to them all is in him. That is why it is 'through him' that we answer Amen to the praise of God"
(II Co. 1:20).

Contents

PART III

Presentation

God is faithful and truthful.

Through faith, we receive beforehand His promised blessings; in trust we wait... and the provident love of the Lord will operate, turning each of His promises into reality.

"The righteous man will live by faith" (He. 10:38a).

Jesus Christ has not changed and never will change (cf. He. 13:8). His words are the same: none of them has been modified, nor His promises, revoked.

"Heaven and earth will pass away, but my words will never pass away" (Mt. 24:35).

You who are downhearted, depressed, discouraged, desolate... try an experiment with the love of God and His power right now!

Open up your heart to Jesus Christ, invite Him to come into your life as your only Savior and Lord. Confess to Him all your sins, repenting them. Ask Jesus to forgive you, to wash you with His precious Blood, and to fill you with His Holy Spirit.

The Holy Spirit is the Spirit of truth. And He will lead you, through the Word of God, to the revelation of the only truth that is Jesus Christ and will enable you to understand the teachings of Jesus – not only with your mind, but with your heart, because with the mind we understand, **but it is with the heart that we must believe**.

Appeal to the **sacraments** of the Church: to **Confession**, to the **Eucharist**; renew the **faith** of your Baptism, intensify your **personal prayer** and be a persistent participant in the celebrations of the Holy Mass.

Now read calmly, meditating, each promise of God to you, in accordance with your specific needs. Remember: God love you! Each promise contained in the Holy Bible is addressed to someone: you... who are a beloved child of God through faith in Jesus Christ.

"To all who did accept him he gave power to become children of God, to all who believe in the name of him" (Jn. 1:12).

The power of God operates through our faith in His infinite love and in the complete confidence by which he will carry out, in our favor, exactly that which is promised in His Word.

Let the promise of the Lord fall into your heart, cherish it with faith and trust, repeat it often in firm voice until it is imprinted upon your mind.

Praise God, for He will fulfill His Word. He will make the Word, which you have accepted with faith and proclaimed

14

with conviction, work in your favor, freeing your heart and filling it with joy and consolation.

Our God lives! He is the Father of all consolation, and none of those who have placed their trust in Him have ever been foresaken. He watches over His Word so that it will be fulfilled – and so it will be in your life.

> *"How good Yahweh is – only taste and see! Happy the man who takes shelter in him"* (Ps. 34:8[33:9]).

God bless you, dear reader, and grant that you may grow constantly in the grace and in the knowledge of Our Lord and Savior Jesus Christ.

Part I

1

What is the Bible?

The Word of God

"All scripture is inspired by God and can profitably be used for teaching, for refuting error, for guiding people's lives and teaching them to be holy."   **II Timothy 3:16**

"At the same time, we must be most careful to remember that the interpretation of scriptural prophecy is never a matter for the individual. Why? Because no prophecy ever came from man's initiative. When men spoke for God it was the Holy Spirit that moved them."   **II Peter 1:20-21**

"It is the spirit that gives life, the flesh has nothing to offer. The words I have spoken to you are spirit and they are life."   **John 6:63**

"The word of God is something alive and active: it cuts like any double-edged sword but more finely: it can slip through the place where the soul is divided from the spirit, or joints from the marrow; it can judge the secret emotions and thoughts."　　　　　　　　　**Hebrews 4:12**

"As the rain and the snow come down from the heavens and do not return without watering the earth, making it yield and giving growth to provide seed for the sower and bread for the eating, so the word that goes from my mouth does not return to me empty, without carrying out my will and succeeding in what it was sent to do."　　　　　　　　　**Isaiah 55:10-11**

"He who rejects me and refuses my words has his judge already: the word itself that I have spoken will be his judge on the last day. For what I have spoken does not come from myself; no, what I was to say, what I had to speak, was commanded by the Father who sent me, and I know that his commands mean eternal life. And therefore what the Father has told me is what I speak."　　　**John 12:48-50**

"Your new birth was not from any mortal seed but from the everlasting word of the living and eternal God."　　　　　　　　　**I Peter 1:23**

"All flesh is grass and its glory like the wild flower's. The grass withers, the flower falls, but the word of the Lord remains for ever. What is this word? It is the Good News that has been brought to you."　　　　　　**I Peter 1:24-25**

"He spoke, and it was created; he commanded, and there it stood."　　　　　　　　　**Psalms 33[32]:9**

"Every word of God is unalloyed, he is the shield of those who take refuge in him."   **Proverbs 30:5**

"Lasting to eternity, your word, Yahweh, unchanging in the heavens."   **Psalms 119[118]:89**

"The word of Yahweh is integrity itself, all he does is done faithfully."   **Psalms 33[32]:4**

"This is my solemn warning to all who hear the prophecies in this book: if anyone adds anything to them, God will add to him every plague mentioned in the book; if anyone cuts anything out of the prophecies in this book, God will cut off his share of the tree of life and of the holy city, which are described in the book."
          Revelation 22:18-19

"Heaven and earth will pass away, but my words will not pass away."   **Mark 13:31**

"Yahweh said, 'Well seen! I too watch over my word to see it fulfilled.'"   **Jeremiah 1:12**

"The angel said to me, 'All that you have written is sure and will come true: the Lord God who gives the spirit to the prophets has sent his angel to reveal to his servants what is soon to take place. Very soon now, I shall be with you again.' Happy are those who treasure the prophetic message of this book."   **Revelation 22:6-7**

Guide

"Have the book of this Law always on your lips; meditate on it day and night, so that you may carefully keep everything that is written in it. Then you will prosper in your dealings, then you will have success. Have I not told you: Be strong and stand firm? Be fearless then, be confident, for go where you will, Yahweh your God is with you."   **Joshua 1:8-9**

"My son, keep my words, and treasure my principles, keep my principles and you will live, keep my teaching as the apple of your eye. Bind these to your fingers, write them on the tablet of your heart."   **Proverbs 7:1-3**

"I will instruct you, and teach you the way to go; I will watch over you and be your adviser."   **Psalms 32[31]:8**

"Listen, my son, take my words to heart, and the years of your life shall be multiplied. I have educated you in the ways of wisdom, I have guided you along the paths of honesty. As you walk, your going will be unhindered, as you run, you will not stumble."   **Proverbs 4:10-12**

"Yahweh, you yourself are my lamp, my God lights up my darkness."   **II Samuel 22:29**

"This by the tender mercy of our God who from on high will bring the rising Sun to visit us, to give light to those who live in darkness and the shadow of death, and to guide our feet into the way of peace."   **Luke 1:78-79**

"Trust wholeheartedly in Yahweh, put no faith in your own perception; in every course you take, have him in mind: he will see that your paths are smooth."
Proverbs 3:5-6

"Put your hope in Yahweh, keep his way, raising you until you make the land your own and see the wicked expelled." **Psalms 37[36]:34**

"To the Jews who believed in him Jesus said: 'If you make my word your home you will indeed be my disciples, you will learn the truth and the truth shall make you free.'" **John 8:31-32**

"Now your word is a lamp to my feet, a light on my path." **Psalms 119[118]:105**

"He guides me by paths of virtue for the sake of his name." **Psalms 23[22]:3**

"When you walk, these will guide you, when you lie down, watch over you, when you wake, talk with you. For this principle is a lamp, this teaching is a light; correction and discipline are the way to life." **Proverbs 6:22-23**

"How can a youth remain pure? By behaving as your word prescribes." **Psalms 119[118]:9**

"I have treasured your promises in my heart, since I have no wish to sin against you." **Psalms 119[118]:11**

"Since your decrees are my delight, your statutes are my counselors." **Psalms 119[118]:24**

"Yahweh guides a man's steps, they are sure, and he takes pleasure in his progress." **Psalms 37[36]:23**

Comfort

"My son, do not forget my teaching, let your heart keep my principles, for these will give you lengthier days, longer years of life, and greater happiness."
Proverbs 3:1-2

"I wait for Yahweh, my soul waits for him, I rely on his promise, my soul relies on the Lord more than a watchman on the coming of dawn." **Psalms 130[129]:5-6**

"Indeed everything that was written long ago in the scriptures was meant to teach us something about hope from the examples scripture gives of how people who did not give up were helped by God." **Romans 15:4**

"My son, pay attention to my words, listen carefully to the words I say; do not let them out of your sight, keep them deep in your heart. They are life to those who grasp them, health for the entire body." **Proverbs 4:20-22**

"I mean to observe your statutes; never abandon me. How can a youth remain pure? By behaving as your word prescribes." **Psalms 119[118]:8-9**

"Had your Law not been my delight I should have perished in my suffering." **Psalms 119[118]:92**

"Universal peace for those who love your Law, no stumbling blocks for them!" **Psalms 119[118]:165**

"There is nothing I cannot master with the help of the One who gives me strength." **Philippians 4:13**

Strength

"Finally, grow strong in the Lord, with the strength of his power."   **Ephesians 6:10**

"That is why you must rely on God's armor, or you will not be able to put up any resistance when the worst happens, or have enough resources to hold your ground."
                                                      Ephesians 6:13

"Now go and inscribe this on a tablet, write it in a book, that it may serve in the time to come as a witness for ever [...] For thus says the Lord Yahweh, the Holy One of Israel: Your salvation lay in conversion and tranquillity, your strength, in complete trust."   **Isaiah 30:8.15a-b**

"He gives strength to the wearied, he strengthens the powerless. Young men may grow tired and weary, youths may stumble, but those who hope in Yahweh renew their strength, they put out wings like eagles. They run and do not grow weary, walk and never tire."   **Isaiah 40:29-31**

"Do not be afraid, for I am with you; stop being anxious and watchful, for I am your God. I give you strength, I bring you help, I uphold you with my victorious right hand."
                                                      Isaiah 41:10

"Be a sheltering rock for me, a walled fortress to save me! For you are my rock, my fortress; for the sake of your name, guide me, lead me!"   **Psalms 31[30]:2b-3**

"There is none like the God of Jeshurun: he rides the heavens to your rescue, rides the clouds in his majesty. The God of old, he is your refuge. Here below, he is the age-old arm driving the enemy before you; it is he who cries, 'Destroy!'"   **Deuteronomy 33:26-28a**

"Yahweh is my rock and my bastion, my deliverer is my God. I take shelter in him, my rock, my shield, my horn of salvation, my stronghold and my refuge. From violence you rescue me. He is to be praised; on Yahweh I call and am saved from my enemies."   **Psalms 18[17]:2-3**

"Thus says Israel's king and his redeemer, Yahweh Sabaoth: I am the first and the last; there is no other God besides me. Have no fear, do not be afraid; have I not told you and revealed it long ago? You are my witnesses, is there any other God besides me? There is no Rock; I know of none."
                    Isaiah 44:6.8

"What comes from my mouth is truth, a word irrevocable: before me every knee shall bend, by me every tongue shall swear, saying, 'From Yahweh alone come victory and strength.'"   **Isaiah 45:23b-24b**

Source of Life

"Yahweh commanded us to observe all these laws and to fear Yahweh our God, so as to be happy for ever and to live, as he has granted us to do until now."

Deuteronomy 6:24

"See, today I set before you life and prosperity, death and disaster. If you obey the commandments of Yahweh your God that I enjoin on you today, if you love Yahweh your God and follow his ways, if you keep his commandments, his laws, his customs, you will live and increase, and Yahweh your God will bless you in the land which you are entering to make your own." **Deuteronomy 30:15-16**

"I call heaven and earth to witness against you today: I set before you life or death, blessing or curse. Choose life, then, so that you and your descendants may live, in the love of Yahweh your God, obeying his voice, clinging to him; for in this your life consists, and on this depends your long stay in the land which Yahweh swore to your fathers Abraham, Isaac and Jacob he would give them."

Deuteronomy 30:19-20

"She is a tree of life for those who hold her fast, those who cling to her live happy lives." **Proverbs 3:18**

"My son, pay attention to my words, listen carefully to the words I say; do not let them out of your sight, keep them deep in your heart. They are life to those who grasp them, health for the entire body." **Proverbs 4:20-22**

"I tell you most solemnly, whoever listens to my words, and believes in the one who sent me, has eternal life; without being brought to judgment he has passed from death to life."   **John 5:24**

"The words I have spoken to you are spirit and they are life."   **John 6:63b**

"Simon Peter answered, 'Lord, who shall we go to? You have the message of eternal life?'" **John 6:68**

"This has been my comfort in my suffering: that your promise gives me life."   **Psalms 119[118]:50**

"I shall never forget your precepts; by these you have kept me alive."   **Psalms 119[118]:93**

"That the various crops are not what nourishes man, but your word which preserves all who trust in you."
                    Wisdom 16:26b-c

Source of Happiness

"For us right living will mean this: to keep and observe all these commandments before Yahweh our God as he has directed us."   **Deuteronomy 6:25**

"She is a tree of life for those who hold her fast, those who cling to her live happy lives." **Proverbs 3:18**

"And now, my sons, listen to me: Happy those who keep my ways!"   **Proverbs 8:32**

"He who listens closely to the word shall find happiness; he who puts his trust in Yahweh is blessed."
                    Proverbs 16:20

"Happy the man who never follows the advice of the wicked, of loiters on the way that sinners take, or sits about with scoffers, but finds his pleasure in the lan of Yahweh, and murmurs his law day and night."
                    Psalms 1:1-2

"Happy, all those who fear Yahweh and follow in his paths. You will eat what your hands have worked for, happiness and prosperity will be yours."
                    Psalms 128[127]:1-2

"Ah, how happy those of blameless life who walk in the Law of Yahweh! How happy those who respect his decrees, and seek him with their whole heart, and, doing no evil walk in his ways!"   **Psalms 119[118]:1-3**

"Happy the man who listens to me, who day after day watches at my gates to guard the portals. For the man who finds me finds life, he will win favor from Yahweh."

Proverbs 8:34-35

"He replied, 'Still happier those who hear the word of God and keep it!'" **Luke 11:28**

"The man who looks steadily at the perfect law of freedom and makes that his habit – not listening and then forgetting, but actively putting it into practice – will be happy in all that he does." **James 1:25**

Source of Wisdom

"You must keep to what you have been taught and know to be true; remember who your teachers were, and how, ever since you were a child, you have known the holy scriptures – from these you can learn the wisdom that leads to salvation through faith in Christ Jesus. All scripture is inspired by God and can profit-ably be used for teaching, for refuting error, for guiding people's lives and teaching them to be holy. This is how the man who is dedicated to God becomes fully equipped and ready for any good work."
II Timothy 3:14-17

"If you wish, my son, you can acquire instruction, if you give your mind to it, subtlety will be yours. If you love listening you will learn, if you lend an ear, wisdom will be yours. [...] Reflect on the injunctions of the Lord, busy yourself at all times with his commandments. He will strengthen your mind, and the wisdom you desire will be granted you."
Ecclesiasticus 6:33-34.37

"As your word unfolds, it gives light, and the simple understand."
Psalms 119[118]:130

"Teach me good sense and knowledge, for I rely on your commandments."
Psalms 119[118]:66

"By your commandment, ever mine, how much wiser you have made me than my enemies! How much subtler than my teachers, through my meditating on your decrees! How much more perceptive than the elders, as a result of my respecting your precepts!"
Psalms 119[118]:98-100

"Your precepts endow me with perception; I hate all deceptive paths." **Psalms 118:104**

"For Yahweh himself is giver of wisdom, from his mouth issue knowledge and discernment." **Proverbs 2:6**

"But still we have a wisdom to offer those who have reached maturity: not a philosophy of our age, it is true, still less of the masters of our age, with are coming to their end. The hidden wisdom of God which we teach in our mysteries is the wisdom that God predestined to be for our glory before the ages began. It is a wisdom that none of the masters of this age have ever known, or they would not have crucified the Lord of Glory." **I Corinthians 2:6-8**

"If there is any one of you who needs wisdom, he must ask God, who gives to all freely and ungrudgingly; it will be given to him." **James 1:5**

"Whereas the wisdom that comes down from above is essentially something pure; it also makes for peace, and is kindly and considerate; it is full of compassion and shows itself by doing good; nor is there any trace of partiality or hypocrisy in it." **James 3:17**

Testament

"And now I commend you to God, and to the word of his grace that has power to build you up and to give you your inheritance among all the sanctified."
Acts 20:32

"I shall deliver you [...] to open their eyes, so that they may turn from darkness to light, from the dominion of Satan to God, and receive, through faith in me, forgiveness of their sins and a share in the inheritance of the sanctified."
Acts 26:17a.18

"The Spirit himself and our spirit bear united witness that we are children of God. And if we are children we are heirs as well: heirs of God and coheirs with Christ, sharing his sufferings so as to share his glory."
Romans 8:16-17

"Merely by belonging to Christ you are the posterity of Abraham, the heirs he was promised."
Galatians 3:29

"And it is this that makes you a son, you are not a slave any more; and if God has made you son, then he has made you heir." **Galatians 4:7**

"And it is in him that we were claimed as God's own, chosen from the beginning, under the predetermined plan of the one who guides all things as he decides by his own will; chosen to be, for his greater glory, the people who would put their hopes in Christ before he came. Now you too, in him, have heard the message of the truth and the good news of your salvation, and have believed it; and you too have been stamped with the seal of the Holy Spirit of the Promise, the pledge of our inheritance which brings freedom for those whom God has taken for his own, to make his glory praised."

Ephesians 1:11-14

"May the God of our Lord Jesus Christ, the Father of glory, give you a spirit of wisdom and perception on what is revealed, to bring you to full knowledge of him. May he enlighten the eyes of your mind so that you can see what hope his call holds for you, what rich glories he has promised the saints will inherit and how infinitely great is the power that he has exercised for us believers. This you can tell strength of his power."   **Ephesians 1:17-19**

"Thanking the Father who has made it possible for you to join the saints and with them to inherit the light."

Colossians 1:12

"Whatever your work is, put your heart into it as if it were for the Lord and not for men, knowing that the Lord will repay you by making you his heirs. It is Christ the Lord that you are serving."   **Colossians 3:23-24**

"He brings a new covenant, as the mediator, only so that the people who were called to an eternal inheritance may actually receive what was promised: his death took place to cancel the sins that infringed the earlier covenant."

Hebrews 9:15

"Blessed be God the Father of our Lord Jesus Christ, who in his great mercy has given us a new birth as his sons, by raising Jesus Christ from the dead, so that we have a sure hope and the promise of an inheritance that can never be spoiled or soiled and never fade away, because it is being kept for you in the heavens." **I Peter 1:3-4**

"There are many rooms in my Father's house; if there were not, I should have told you. I am going now to prepare a place for you, and after I have gone and prepared you a place, I shall return to take you with me; so that where I am you may be too." **John 14:2-3**

"And however many the promises God made, the Yes to them all is in him. That is why it is 'through him' that we answer amen to the praise of God." **II Corinthians 1:20**

"Then the King will say to those on his right hand, 'Come, you whom my Father has blessed, take for your heritage the kingdom prepared for you since the foundation of the world.'" **Mattew 25:34**

"There is no need to be afraid, little flock, for it has pleased your Father to give you the kingdom." **Luke 12:32**

2

Who is God?

Creator

"In the beginning God created the heavens and the earth."   **Genesis 1:1**

"God created man in the image of himself, in the image of God he created him, male and female he created them."
Genesis 1:27

"That day, man will look to his creator and his eyes will turn to the Holy One of Israel."   **Isaiah 17:7**

"I am Yahweh, your Holy One, the creator of Israel, your king."   **Isaiah 43:15**

"By his power he made the earth, by his wisdom set the world firm, by his discernment spread out the heavens."

Jeremiah 10:12

"Since the God who made the world and everything in it is himself Lord of heaven and earth, he does not make his home in shrines made by human hands. Nor is he dependent on anything that human hands can do for him, since he can never be in need of anything; on the contrary, it is he who gives everything – including life and breath – to everyone. From one single stock he not only created the whole human race so that they could occupy the entire earth, but he decreed how long each nation should flourish and what the boundaries of its territory should be."

Acts 17:24-26

Eternal

"Did you not know? Had you not heard? Yahweh is an everlasting God, he created the boundaries of the earth. He does not grow tired or weary, his understanding is beyond fathoming."   **Isaiah 40:28**

"But Yahweh is the true God. He is the living God, the everlasting King."   **Jeremiah 10:10a**

"Yahweh has appeared to him from afar: I have loved you with an everlasting love, so I am constant in my affection for you."   **Jeremiah 31:3**

"And sovereignty and kingship, and the splendors of all the kingdoms under heaven will be given to the people of the saints of the Most High. His sovereignty is an eternal sovereignty and every empire will serve and obey him."   **Daniel 7:27**

"To the eternal King, the undying, invisible and only God, be honor and glory for ever and ever. Amen."   **I Timothy 1:17**

"It is all that is good, everything that is perfect, which is given us from above; it comes down from the Father of all light; with him there is no such thing as alteration, no shadow of a change."   **James 1:17**

Omniscient

"Do not speak and speak with haughty words, let not arrogance come from your mouth. For Yahweh is an all-knowing God and his is the weighing of deeds."
I Samuel 2:3

"We teach what scripture calls: the things that no eye has seen and no ear has heard, things beyond the mind of man, all that God has prepared for those who love him. These are the very things that God has revealed to us through the Spirit, for the Spirit reaches the depths of everything, even the depths of God."   **I Corinthians 2:9-10**

"Yahweh, you examine me and know me, you know if I am standing or sitting, you read my thoughts from far away, whether I walk or lie down, you are watching, you know every detail of my conduct. The word is not even on my tongue, Yahweh, before you know all about it; close behind and close in front you fence me around, shielding me with your hand. Such knowledge is beyond my understanding, a height to which my mind cannot attain.

[...] It was you who created my inmost self, and put me together in my mother's womb; for all these mysteries I thank you: for the wonder of myself, for the wonder of your works. You know me through and through, from having watched my bones take shape when I was being formed in secret, knitted together in the limbo of the womb. You had scrutinized my every action, all were recorded in your book, my days listed and determined, even before the first of them occurred.

God, how hard it is to grasp your thoughts! How impossible to count them! I could no more count them than I could the sand, and suppose I could, you would still be with me."   **Psalms 139[138]:1-6.13-18**

"Then he said to him a third time, 'Simon son of John, do you love me?' Peter was upset that he asked him the third time, 'Do you love me?' and said, 'Lord, you know everything; you know I love you.' Jesus said to him, 'Feed my sheep.'"   **John 21:17**

Omnipresent

"Where could I go to escape your spirit? Where could I flee from your presence? If I climb the heavens, you are there, there too, if I lie in Sheol. If I flew to the point of sunrise, or westward across the sea, your hand would still be guiding me, your right hand holding me. If I asked darkness to cover me, and light to become night around me, that darkness would not be dark to you, night would be as light as day."
Psalms 139[138]:7-12

"You alone bear the name Yahweh, Most High over the whole world." **Psalms 83[82]:18b-c**

"You whose imperishable spirit is in all."
Wisdom 12:1

"The spirit of the Lord, indeed, fills the whole world, and that which holds all things together knows every word that is said." **Wisdom 1:7**

Omnipotent

"If you live in the shelter of Elyon and make your home in the shadow of Shaddai, you can say to Yahweh, 'My refuge, my fortress, my God in whom I trust!'"

Psalms 91[90]:1-2

"When Abram was ninety-nine years old Yahweh appeared to him and said, 'I am El Shaddai. Bear yourself blameless in my presence?'"   **Genesis 17:1**

"God spoke to Moses and said to him, 'I am Yahweh. To Abraham and Isaac and Jacob I appeared as El Shaddai; I did not make myself known to them by my name Yahweh.'"

Exodus 6:1d-3

"Happy indeed the man whom God corrects! Then do not refuse this lesson from Shaddai."

Job 5:17

"If you return, humbled, to Shaddai and drive all injustice from your tents, if you reckon gold as dust and Ophir as the pebbles of the torrent, then you will find Shaddai worth bars of gold or silver piled in heaps. Then Shaddai will be all your delight." **Job 22:23-26a**

"He, Shaddai, is far beyond our reach. Supreme in power, in equity, excelling in justice, yet no oppressor."

Job 37:23

"'The words are your own,' answered Jesus. 'Moreover, I tell you that from this time onward you will see the Son of Man seated at the right hand of the Power and coming on the clouds of heaven.'" **Matthew 26:64**

"The spirit of those who fear the Lord can survive, for their hope is in someone with power to save them. The man who fears the Lord will not be fainthearted, will not be daunted since the Lord is his hope. Happy the soul of the man who fears the Lord." **Ecclesiasticus 34:14-15**

"'I am the Alpha and the Omega,' says the Lord God, who is, who was, and who is to come, the Almighty." **Revelation 1:8**

"Each of the four animals had six wings and had eyes all the way around as well as inside; and day and night they never stopped singing: 'Holy, Holy, Holy is the Lord God, the Almighty; he was, he is and he is to come.'" **Revelation 4:8**

"We give thanks to you, Almighty Lord God, He-Is-and-He-Was, for using your great power and beginning your reign." **Revelation 11:17b**

"They were singing the hymn of Moses, the servant of God, and of the Lamb: 'How great and wonderful are all your works, Lord God Almighty; just and true are all your ways, King of nations.'" **Revelation 15:3**

"I heard the altar itself say, 'Truly, Lord God Almighty, the punishments you give are true and just.'" **Revelation 16:7**

"I seemed to hear the voices of a huge crowd, like the sound of the ocean or the great roar of thunder, answering, 'Alleluia! The reign of the Lord our God Almighty has begun.'" **Revelation 19:6**

"I saw that there was no temple in the city since the Lord God Almighty and the Lamb were themselves the temple." **Revelation 21:22**

Spirit

"God is spirit, and those who worship must worship in spirit and truth."   **John 4:24**

"We teach what scripture calls: the things that no eye has seen and no ear has heard, things beyond the mind of man, all that God has prepared for those who love him. These are the very things that God has revealed to us through the Spirit, for the Spirit reaches the depths of everything, even the depths of God. After all, the depths of a man can only be known by his own spirit, not by any other man, and in the same way the depths of God can only be known by the Spirit of God."   **I Corinthians 2:9-11**

"Now the earth was a formless void, there was darkness over the deep, and God's spirit hovered over the water."
Genesis 1:2

"Where could I go to escape your spirit? Where could I flee from your presence?"   **Psalms 139[138]:7**

"On him the spirit of Yahweh rests, a spirit of wisdom and insight, a spirit of counsel and power, a spirit of knowledge and of the fear of Yahweh."
Isaiah 11:2

"The spirit of the Lord Yahweh has been given to me, for Yahweh has anointed me. He has sent me to bring good

46

news to the poor, to bind up hearts that are broken; to proclaim liberty to captives, freedom to those in prison."

Isaiah 61:1

"I shall put my spirit in you, and make you keep my laws and sincerely respect my observances."

Ezekiel 36:27

"You will know that I am Yahweh and I shall put my spirit in you, and you will live, and I shall resettle you on your own soil; and you will know that I, Yahweh, have said and done this – it is the Lord Yahweh who speaks."

Ezekiel 37:13a.14

"After this I will pour out my spirit on all mankind."

Joel 3:1

"Jesus replied: 'I tell you most solemnly, unless a man is born through water and the Spirit, he cannot enter the kingdom of God: what is born of the flesh is flesh; what is born of the Spirit is spirit.'"   **John 3:5-6**

Holy

"For it is I, Yahweh, who am your God. You have been sanctified and have become holy because I am holy."
Leviticus 11:44a

"Yes, it is I, Yahweh, who brought you out of Egypt to be your God: you therefore must be holy because I am holy."
Leviticus 11:45

"Yahweh spoke to Moses; he said: 'Speak to the whole community of the sons of Israel and say to them: Be holy, for I, Yahweh your God, am holy.'"   **Leviticus 19:1-2**

"Be consecrated to me, because I, Yahweh, am holy, and I will set you apart from all these peoples so that you may be mine."   **Leviticus 20:26**

"There is none as holy as Yahweh, (indeed, there is no one but you) no rock like our God."
I Samuel 2:2

"And they cried out one to another in this way, 'Holy, holy, holy, is Yahweh Sabaoth. His glory fills the whole earth.'"
Isaiah 6:3

"Cry out for joy and gladness, you dwellers in Zion, for great in the midst of you is the Holy One of Israel."
Isaiah 12:6

"Do not be afraid, Jacob, poor worm, Israel, puny mite. I will help you – it is Yahweh who speaks – the Holy One of Israel is your redeemer." **Isaiah 41:14**

"Ephraim, how could I part with you? Israel, how could I give you up? How could I treat you like Admah, or deal with you like Zeboiim? My heart recoils from it, my whole being trembles at the thought. I will not give rein to my fierce anger, I will not destroy Ephraim again, for I am God, not man: I am the Holy One in your midst and have no wish to destroy." **Hosea 11:8-9**

"We believe; we know that you are the Holy One of God." **John 6:69**

"Be holy in all you do, since it is the Holy One who has called you, and scripture says: Be holy, for I am holy." **I Peter 1:15-16**

"Each of the four animals had six wings and had eyes all the way around as well as inside; and day and night they never stopped singing: 'Holy, Holy, Holy is the Lord God, the Almighty; he was, he is and he is to come.'" **Revelation 4:8**

"Who would not revere and praise your name, O Lord? You alone are holy, and all the pagans will come and adore you for the many acts of justice you have shown." **Revelation 15:4**

"Then I heard the angel of water say, 'You are the holy He-Is-and-He-Was, the Just One, and this is a just punishment.'" **Revelation 16:5**

Love

"Anyone who fails to love can never have known God, because God is love." **I John 4:8**

"We ourselves have known and put our faith in God's love toward ourselves. God is love and anyone who lives in love lives in God, and God lives in him."
I John 4:16

"God loved us with so much love that he was generous with his mercy: when we were dead through our sins, he brought us to life with Chris – it is through grace that you have been saved." **Ephesians 2:4-5**

"What proves that God loves us is that Christ died for us while we were still sinners." **Romans 5:8**

"Blessed be the God and Father of our Lord Jesus Christ, a gentle Father and the God of all consolation."
II Corinthians 1:3

"My dear people, let us love one another since love comes from God and everyone who loves is begotten by God and knows God." **I John 4:7**

One and Three

(A single God in Three Distinct Persons)

"Listen, Israel: Yahweh our God is the one Yahweh."
Deuteronomy 6:4

"See now that I, I am He, and beside me there is no other god." **Deuteronomy 32:39a**

"Still for us there is one God, the Father from whom all things come and for whom we exist."
I Corinthians 8:6a

"And one God who is Father of all, over all, through all and within all." **Ephesians 4:6**

"Jesus replied, 'This is the first: Listen Israel, the Lord our God is the one Lord.'" **Mark 12:29**

"So you should pray like this: 'Our Father in heaven, may your name be held holy.'" **Matthew 6:9**

"Jesus said to her, 'Do not cling to me, because I have not yet ascended to the Father. But go and find the brothers, and tell them: I am ascending to my Father and your Father, to my God and your God.'" **John 20:17**

"Well then, about eating food sacrificed to idols: we know that idols do not really exist in the world and that there is no god but the One."   **I Corinthians 8:4**

"'The Holy Spirit will come upon you,' the angel answered, and the power of the Most High will cover you with its shadow. And so the child will be holy and will be called Son of God."   **Luke 1:35**

"When all the people had been baptized and while Jesus after his own baptism was at prayer, heaven opened and the Holy Spirit descended on him in bodily shape, like a dove. And a voice came from heaven, 'You are my Son, the Beloved; my favor rests on you.'"   **Luke 3:21-22**

"If you love me you will keep my commandments. I shall ask the Father, and he will give you another Advocate to be with you for ever."   **John 14:15-16**

"When the Advocate comes, whom I shall send to you from the Father, the Spirit of truth who issues from the Father, he will be my witness."   **John 15:26**

"Go, therefore, make disciples of all the nations; baptize them in the name of the Father and of the Son and of the Holy Spirit."   **Matthew 28:19**

"The grace of the Lord Jesus Christ, the love of God and the fellowship of the Holy Spirit be with you all."
                    II Corinthians 13:13

3

Who is Jesus Christ?

Our Savior

"Yes, God loved the world so much that he gave his only Son, so that everyone who believes in him may not be lost but may have eternal life."   **John 3:16**

"It was not because he was concerned with any righteous actions we might have done ourselves; it was for no reason except his own compassion that he saved us, by means of the cleansing water of rebirth and by renewing us with the Holy Spirit which he has so generously poured over us through Jesus Christ our Savior."   **Titus 3:5-6**

"We ourselves saw and we testify that the Father sent his Son as savior of the world."   **I John 4:14**

"Now we no longer believe because of what you told us; we have heard him ourselves and we know that he really is the savior of the world."   **John 4:42b**

"The Son of Man has come to seek out and save what was lost."   **Luke 19:10**

"God never meant us to experience the Retribution, but to win salvation through our Lord Jesus Christ."
I Thessalonians 5:9

"This is the stone rejected by you the builders, but which has proved to be the keystone. For of all the names in the world given to men, this is the only one by which we can be saved."   **Acts 4:11-12**

"For there is only one God, and there is only one mediator between God and mankind, himself a man, Christ Jesus, who sacrificed himself as a ransom for them all."
I Timothy 2:5-6a

"So I bear it all for the sake of those who are chosen, so that in the end they may have the salvation that is in Christ Jesus and the eternal glory that comes with it."
II Timothy 2:10

"But having been made perfect, he became for all who obey him the source of eternal salvation."
Hebrews 5:9

"Today in the town of David a savior has been born to you; he is Christ the Lord."   **Luke 2:11**

"It was the God of our ancestors who raised up Jesus, but it was you who had him executed by hanging on a tree. By his own right hand God has now raised him up to be leader and savior, to give repentance and forgiveness of sins through him to Israel."   **Acts 5:30-31**

"To keep his promise, God has raised up for Israel one of David's descendants, Jesus, as Savior."
Acts 13:23

"For us, our homeland is in heaven, and from heaven comes the Savior we are waiting for, the Lord Jesus Christ."
Philippians 3:20

"Since as Christ is head of the Church and saves the whole body, so is a husband the head of his wife."
Ephesians 5:23

"That is a saying that you can rely on and nobody should doubt it. I mean that the point of all our toiling and battling is that we have put our trust in the living God and he is the savior of the whole human race but particularly of all believers."   **I Timothy 4:9-10**

"God who has saved us and called us to be holy – not because of anything we ourselves have done but for his own purpose and by his own grace. This grace had already been granted to us, in Christ Jesus, before the beginning of time, but it has only been revealed by the Appearing of our Savior Christ Jesus. He abolished death, and he has proclaimed life and immortality through the Good News."
II Timothy 1:9-10

The Son of God Incarnate

"Listen! You are to conceive and bear a son, and you must name him Jesus. He will be great and will be called Son of the Most High. The Lord God will give him the throne of his ancestor David; he will rule over the House of Jacob for ever and his reign will have no end."

Luke 1:31-33

"'The Holy Spirit will come upon you,' the angel answered, 'and the power of the Most High will cover you with its shadow. And so the child will be holy and will be called Son of God.'" **Luke 1:35**

"Now all this took place to fulfill the words spoken by the Lord through the prophet: The virgin will conceive and give birth to a son and they will call him Immanuel, a name which means 'God-is-with-us.'" **Matthew 1:22-23**

"When the appointed time came, God sent his Son, born of a woman, born a subject of the Law, to redeem the subjects of the Law and to enable us to be adopted as sons."

Galatians 4:4-5

"God has done what the Law, because of our unspiritual nature, was unable to do. God dealt with sin by sending his own Son in a body as physical as any sinful body, and in that body God condemned sin. He did this in order that the Law's just demands might be satisfied in us, who behave not as our unspiritual nature but as the spirit dictates."

Romans 8:3-4

"Yes, God loved the world so much that he gave his only Son, so that everyone who believes in him may not be lost but may have eternal life. For God sent his Son into the world not to condemn the world, but so that through him the world might be saved. No one who believes in him will be condemned; but whoever refuses to believe is condemned already, because he has refused to believe in the name of God's only Son." **John 3:16-18**

"As soon as Jesus was baptized he came up from the water, and suddenly the heavens opened and he saw the Spirit of God descending like a dove and coming down on him. And a voice spoke from heaven, 'This is my Son, the Beloved; my favor rests on him.'" **Matthew 3:16-17**

"Yes, I have seen and I am the witness that he is the Chosen One of God." **John 1:34**

"Nathanael answered, 'Rabbi, you are the Son of God, you are the King of Israel.'" **John 1:49**

"Devils too came out of many people, howling, 'You are the Son of God.' But he rebuked them and would not allow them to speak because they knew that he was the Christ." **Luke 4:41**

"Catching sight of Jesus he gave a shout, fell at his feet and cried out at the top of his voice, 'What do you want with me, Jesus, son of the Most High God? I implore you, do not torture me?'" **Luke 8:28**

"The men in the boat bowed down before him and said, 'Truly, you are the Son of God.'" **Matthew 14:33**

"Then Simon Peter spoke up, 'You are the Christ,' he said, 'the Son of the living God.'" **Matthew 16:16**

"He was still speaking when suddenly a bright cloud covered them with shadow, and from the cloud there came a voice which said, 'This is my Son, the Beloved; he enjoys my favor. Listen to him.'" **Matthew 17:5**

"'We have a Law,' the Jews replied, 'and according to that Law he ought to die, because he has claimed to be the Son of God.'" **John 19:7**

"Yet you say to someone the Father has consecrated and sent into the world, 'You are blaspheming,' because he says, 'I am the Son of God.'" **Jonh 10:36**

"Then they all said, 'So you are the Son of God then?' He answered, 'It is you who say I am.'"
Luke 22:70

"Meanwhile the centurion, together with the others guarding Jesus, had seen the earthquake and all that was taking place, and they were terrified and said, In truth this was a son of God.'" **Matthew 27:54**

"[This Evangel God] promised long ago through his prophets in the scriptures. This news is about the Son of God who, according to the human nature he took, was a descendant of David: it is about Jesus Christ our Lord who, in the order of the spirit, the spirit of holiness that was in him, was proclaimed Son of God in all his power through his resurrection from the dead." **Romans 1:2-4**

"As we are in union with the Father and with his Son Jesus Christ."   **I John 1:3b**

"It is true that Moses was faithful in the house of God, as a servant, acting as witness to the things which were to be divulged later; but Christ was faithful as a son, and as the master in the house."   **Hebrews 3:5-6a**

"Who can overcome the world? Only the man who believes that Jesus is the Son of God."

I John 5:5

"He began preaching in the synagogues, 'Jesus is the Son of God.'"   **Acts 9:20**

"It was not any cleverly invented myths that we were repeating when we brought you the knowledge of the power and the coming of our Lord Jesus Christ; we had seen his majesty for ourselves. He was honored and glorified by God the Father, when the Sublime Glory itself spoke to him and said, 'This is my Son, the Beloved; he enjoys my favor.'"

II Peter 1:16-17

"We ourselves saw and we testify that the Father sent his Son as savior of the world. If anyone acknowledges that Jesus is the Son of God, God lives in him, and he in God."

I John 4:14-15

"We know, too, that the Son of God has come, and has given us the power to know the true God. We are in the true God, as we are in his Son, Jesus Christ. This is the true God, this is eternal life."   **I John 5:20**

Our Lord

"For this reason the whole House of Israel can be certain that God has made this Jesus whom you crucified both Lord and Christ." **Acts 2:36**

"And that every tongue should acclaim Jesus Christ as Lord, to the glory of God the Father." **Philippians 2:11**

"If your lips confess that Jesus is Lord and if you believe in your heart that God raised him from the dead, then you will be saved." **Romans 10:9**

"Why do you call me, 'Lord, Lord' and not do what I say?" **Luke 6:46**

"If we live, we live for the Lord; and if we die, we die for the Lord, so that alive or dead we belong to the Lord." **Romans 14:8**

"So the Son of Man is master even of the sabbath." **Mark 2:28**

"Today in the town of David a savior has been born to you; he is Christ the Lord." **Luke 2:11**

"Who said to them: 'Yes, it is true. The Lord has risen and has appeared to Simon.'" **Luke 24:34**

"Simon Peter answered, 'Lord, who shall we go to? You have the message of eternal life.'" **John 6:68**

"You call me Master and Lord, and rightly; so I am. If I, then, the Lord and Master, have washed your feet, you should wash each other's feet." **John 13:13-14**

"Thomas replied, 'My Lord and my God!'"
John 20:28

"When Martha heard that Jesus had come she went to meet him. Mary remained sitting in the house. Martha said to Jesus, 'If you had been here, my brother would not have died.'" **John 11:20-21**

"As they were stoning him, Stephen said in invocation, 'Lord Jesus, receive my spirit.' Then he knelt down and said aloud, 'Lord, do not hold this sin against them'; and with these words he fell asleep." **Acts 7:59-60**

"Remember, we believe that we are saved in the same way as they are: through the grace of the Lord Jesus."
Atcs 15:11

"They tolds him, 'Become a believer in the Lord Jesus, and you will be saved, and your household too.'"
Acts 16:31

"When they heard this, they were baptized in the name of the Lord Jesus." **Acts 19:5**

"To this he replied, 'What are you trying to do – weaken my resolution by your tears? For my part, I am ready not only to be tied up but even to die in Jerusalem for the name of the Lord Jesus.'"　　　　　**Acts 21:13**

"It makes no distinction between Jew and Greek: all belong to the same Lord who is rich enough, however many ask his help, for everyone who calls on the name of the Lord will be saved (Jl 3:5)."　　　　　**Romans 10:12-13**

"Let your armor be the Lord Jesus Christ; forget about satisfying your bodies with all their cravings."
　　　　　Romans 13:14

"This explains why Christ both died and came to life, it was so that he might be Lord both of the dead and of the living."　　　　　**Romans 14:9**

"It is for that reason that I want you to understand that on the one hand no one can be speaking under the influence of the Holy Spirit and say, 'Curse Jesus,' and on the other hand, no one can say, 'Jesus is Lord,' unless he is under the influence of the Holy Spirit."　　　**I Corinthians 12:3**

"So let us thank God for giving us the victory through our Lord Jesus Christ."　　　　　**I Corinthians 15:57**

"For it is not ourselves that we are preaching, but Christ Jesus as the Lord, and ourselves as your servants for Jesus' sake."　　　　　**II Corinthians 4:5**

"Remember how generous the Lord Jesus was: he was rich, but he became poor for your sake, to make you rich out of his poverty." **II Corinthians 8:9**

"And never say or do anything except in the name of the Lord Jesus, giving thanks to God the Father through him." **Colossians 3:17**

"And may he so confirm your hearts in holiness that you may be blameless in the sight of our God and Father when our Lord Jesus Christ comes with all his saints." **I Thessalonians 3:13**

"God never meant us to experience the Retribution, but to win salvation through our Lord Jesus Christ." **I Thessalonians 5:9**

"Of doing all that you have been told, with no faults or failures, until the Appearing of our Lord Jesus Christ." **I Timothy 6:14**

"The one who guarantees these revelations repeats his promise: I shall indeed be with you soon. Amen; come, Lord Jesus. May the grace of the Lord Jesus be with you all. Amen." **Revelation 22:20-21**

Our Liberator

"To the Jews who believed in him Jesus said: 'If you make my word your home you will indeed be my disciples, you will learn the truth and the truth shall make you free.'"
John 8:31-32

"So if the Son makes you free, you will be free indeed."
John 8:36

"The spirit of the Lord Yahweh has been given to me, for Yahweh has anointed me. He has sent me to bring good news news to the poor, to bind up hearts that are broken; to proclaim liberty to captives, freedom to those in prison."
Isaiah 61:1

"Yahweh is my rock and my bastion, my deliverer is my God. I take shelter in him, my rock, my shield, my horn of salvation, my stronghold and my refuge. From violence you rescue me." **Psalms 18[17]:2**

"To me, poor wretch, come quickly, Lord! My helper, my savior, my God, come and do not delay!"
Psalms 40[39]:17

"Blessed be Yahweh, [...] my love, my bastion, my citadel, my savior, I shelter behind him, my shield, he makes the nations submit to me." **Psalms 144[143]:1a.2**

"Is that law of the spirit of life in Christ Jesus has set you free from the law of sin and death."
Romans 8:2

"Now this Lord is the Spirit, and where the Spirit of the Lord is, there is freedom." **II Corinthians 3:17**

"When Christ freed us, he meant us to remain free. Stand firm, therefore, and do not submit again to the yoke of slavery." **Galatians 5:1**

The Love of God for Us

"But what proves that God loves us is that Christ died for us while we were still sinners." **Romans 5:8**

"Yes, God loved the world so much that he gave his only Son, so that everyone who believes in him may not be lost but may have eternal life." **John 3:16**

"God's love for us was revealed when God sent into the world his only Son so that we could have life through him; this is the love I mean: not our love for God, but God's love for us when he sent his Son to be the sacrifice that takes our sins away." **I John 4:9-10**

"As the Father has loved me, so I have loved you. Remain in my love. [...] A man can have no greater love than to lay down his life for his friends." **John 15:9.13**

"So that Christ may live in your hearts through faith, and then, planted in love and built on love, you will with all the saints have strength to grasp the breadth and the length, the height and the depth; until, knowing the love of Christ, which is beyond all knowledge, you are filled with the utter fullness of God." **Ephesians 3:17-19**

"Anybody who receives my commandments and keeps them will be one who loves me; and anybody who loves me will be loved by my Father, and I shall love him and show myself to him." **John 14:21**

"He was still speaking when suddenly a bright cloud covered them with shadow, and from the cloud there came a voice which said, 'This is my Son, the Beloved; he enjoys my favor. Listen to him.'"   **Matthew 17:5**

"This has taught us love – that he gave up his life for us; and we, too, ought to give up our lives for our brothers."
I John 3:16

"Because God wanted all perfection to be found in him and all things to be reconciled through him and for him, everything in heaven and everything on earth, when he made peace by his death on the cross." **Colossians 1:19-20**

Our Forgiveness

"In whom, through his blood, we gain our freedom, the forgivenes of our sins. Such is the richness of the grace which he has showered on us in all wisdom and insight."
Ephesians 1:7-8

"I am writing this, my children, to stop you sinning; but if anyone should sin, we have our advocate with the Father, Jesus Christ, who is just; he is the sacrifice that takes our sins away, and not only ours, but the whole world's."
I John 2:1-2

"Bear with one another; forgive each other as soon as a quarrel begins. The Lord has forgiven you; now you must do the same." **Colossians 3:13**

"You were dead, because you were sinners and had not been circumcised: he has brought you to life with him, he has forgiven us all our sins." **Colossians 2:13**

"This is what we have heard from him, and the message that we are announcing to you: God is light; there is no darkness in him at all. But if we live our lives in the light, as he is in the light, we are in union with one another, and the blood of Jesus, his Son, purifies us from all sin."
I John 1:5.7

"Then some people appeared, bringing him a paralytic stretched out on a bed. Seeing their faith, Jesus said to the paralytic, 'Courage, my child, your sins are forgiven.'"
Matthew 9:2

"Then he took a cup, and when he had returned thanks he gave it to them. 'Drink all of you from this,' he said, 'for this is my blood, the blood of the covenant, which is to be poured out for many for the forgiveness of sins.'"

Matthew 26:27-28

"Seeing their faith he said, 'My friend, your sins are forgiven you.'" **Luke 5:20**

"The next day, seeing Jesus coming toward him, John said, 'Look, there is the lamb of God that takes away the sin of the world.'" **John 1:29**

"'You must repent,' Peter answered, 'and every one of you must be baptized in the name of Jesus Christ for the forgiveness of your sins, and you will receive the gift of the Holy Spirit.'"

Acts 2:38

"The reason, therefore, why those who are in Christ Jesus are not condemned, is that the law of the spirit of life in Christ Jesus has set you free from the law of sin and death."

Romans 8:1-2

Our Peace

"For he is the peace between us."

Ephesians 2:14a

"For there is a child born for us, a son given to us and dominion is laid on his shoulders; and this is the name they give him: Wonder Counselor, Mighty God, Eternal Father, Prince of Peace."　　　　**Isaiah 9:5**

"The God of peace will soon crush Satan beneath your feet."　　　　**Romans 16:20a**

"Keep doing all the things that you learned from me and have been taught by me and have heard or seen that I do. Then the God of peace will be with you."

Philippians 4:9

"So far then we have seen that, through our Lord Jesus Christ, by faith we are judged righteous and at peace with God."　　　　**Romans 5:1**

"And may the peace of Christ reign in your hearts, because it is for this that you were called together as parts of one body. Always be thankful."　　**Colossians 3:15**

"Peace I bequeath to you, my own peace I give you, a peace the world cannot give, this is my gift to you. Do not let your hearts be troubled or afraid." **John 14:27**

"I have told you all this so that you may find peace in me. In the world you will have trouble, but be brave: I have conquered the world." **John 16:33**

"They were still talking about all this when he himself stood among them and said to them, 'Peace be with you!'"
Luke 24:36

"There is no need to worry; but if there is anything you need, pray for it, asking God for it with prayer and thanksgiving, and that peace of God, which is so much greater than we can understand, will guard your hearts nd your thoughts, in Christ Jesus." **Philippians 4:6-7**

"In the evening of that same day, the first day of the week, the doors were closed in the room where the disciples were, for fear of the Jews. Jesus came and stood among them. He said to them, 'Peace be with you,' and showed them his hands and his side. The disciples were filled with joy when they saw the Lord, and he said to them again, 'Peace be with you. As the Father sent me, so am I sending you?'"
John 20:19-21

"And for anyone who is in Christ, there is a new creation; the old creation has gone, and now the new one is here. It is all God's work. It was God who reconciled us to himself through Christ and gave us the work of handing on this rec-onciliation. In other words, God in Christ was reconciliation the world to himself, not holding men's faults against them, and he has entrusted to us the news that they are reconciled."
II Corinthians 5:17-19

Our Justice

"But God has made you members of Christ Jesus and by God's doing he has become our wisdom, and our virtue, and our holiness, and our freedom."

I Corinthians 1:30

"For him I have accepted the loss of everything, and I look on everything as so much rubbish if only I can have Christ and be given a place in him. I am no longer trying for perfection by my own efforts, the perfection that comes from the Law, but I want only the perfection that comes through faith in Christ, and is from God and based on faith."

Philippians 3:8b-9

"It is the same justice of God that comes through faith to everyone, Jew and pagan alike, who believes in Jesus Christ. Both Jew and pagan sinned and forfeited God's glory, and both are justified through the free gift of his grace by being redeemed in Christ Jesus." **Romans 3:22-24**

"If it is certain that death reigned over everyone as the consequence of one man's fall, it is even more certain that one man, Jesus Christ, will cause everyone to reign in life who receives the free gift that he does not deserve, of being made righteous." **Romans 5:17**

"God has done what the Law, because of our unspiritual nature, was unable to do. God dealt with sin by sending his own Son in a body as physical as any sinful body, and in that body God condemned sin. He did this in order that the Law's just demands might be satisfied in us, who behave not as our unspiritual nature but as the spirit dictates."

Romans 8:3-4

"If your lips confess that Jesus is Lord and if you believe in your heart that God raised him from the dead, then you will be saved. By believing from the heart you are made righteous; by confessing with your lips you are saved."

Romans 10:9-10

Our Security

"Since Yahweh will be your guarantor, he will keep your steps from the snare." **Proverbs 3:26**

"The sheep that belong to me listen to my voice; I know them and they follow me. [...] The Father who gave them to me is greater than anyone, and no one can steal from the Father." **John 10:27.29**

"For I am certain of this: neither death nor life, no angel, no prince, nothing that exists, nothing still to come, not any power, or height or depth, nor any created thing, can ever come between us and the love of God made visible in Christ Jesus our Lord." **Romans 8:38-39**

"All that the Father gives me will come to me, and whoever comes to me I shall not turn him away."
John 6:37

"Now the will of him who sent me is that I should lose nothing of all that he has given to me, and that I should raise it up on the last day." **John 6:39**

"Ah, how goodness and kindness pursue me, every day of my life; my home, the house of Yahweh, as long as I live!"
Psalms 23[22]:6

"I will not leave you orphans; I will come back to you."
John 14:18

"And know that I am with you always; yes, to the end of time." **Matthew 28:20b**

"Unload all your worries on to him, since he is looking after you." **I Peter 5:7**

"I rescue all who cling to me, I protect whoever knows my name, I answer everyone who invokes me, I am with them when they are in trouble; I bring them safety and honor. I give them life, long and full, and show them how I can save." **Psalms 91[90]:14-16**

"I love you, Yahweh, my strength (my savior, you rescue me from violence). Yahweh is my rock and my bastion, my deliverer is my God. I take shelter in him, my rock, my shield, my horn of salvation, my stronghold and my refuge. From violence you rescue me. He is to be praised; on Yahweh I call and am saved from my enemies." **Psalms 18[17]:1-3**

"God is our shelter, ever ready to help in time of trouble, so we shall not be afraid when the earth gives way when mountains tumble into the depths of the sea, and its waters roar and seethe, the mountains tottering as it heaves. (Yahweh Sabaoth is on our side, our citadel, the God of Jacob!)" **Psalms 46[45]:1-3**

"Hard pressed, I invoked Yahweh, he heard me and came to my relief. With Yahweh on my side, I fear nothing: what can man do to me? With Yahweh on my side, best help of all, I can triumph over my enemies. I would rather take refuge in Yahweh than rely on men; I would rather take refuge in Yahweh than rely on princes."

Psalms 118[117]:5-9

"The guardian of Israel does not doze or sleep. Yahweh guards you, shades you. With Yahweh at your right hand sun cannot strike you down by day, nor moon at night. Yahweh guards you from harm, he guards your lives, he guards you leaving, coming back, now and for always."

Psalms 121[120]:4-8

"Those who trust in Yahweh are like Mount Zion, unshakable, standing for ever."   **Psalms 125[124]:1**

Our Brother

"But to all who did accept him he gave power to become children of God, to all who believe in the name of him."
John 1:12

"So you should pray like this: 'Our Father in heaven, may your name be held holy.'" **Matthew 6:9**

"Jesus said to her, 'Do not cling to me, because I have not yet ascended to the Father. But go and find the brothers, and tell them: I am ascending to my Father and your Father, to my God and your God.'" **John 20:17**

"And you are, all of you, sons of God through faith in Christ Jesus." **Galatians 3:26**

"Anyone who does the will of my Father in heaven, he is my brother and sister and mother."
Matthew 12:50

"They are the ones he chose specially long ago and intended to become true images of his Son, so that his Son might be the eldest of many brothers."
Romans 8:29

"Think of the love that Father has lavished on us, by letting us be called God's children; and that is what we are."
I John 3:1a

"The proof that you are sons is that God has sent the Spirit of his Son into our hearts: the Spirit that cries, 'Abba, Father,' and it is this that makes you a son, you are not a slave any more; and if God has made you son, then he has made you heir."   **Galatians 4:6-7**

"The Spirit himself and our spirit bear united witness that we are children of God. And if we are children we are heirs as well: heirs of God and coheirs with Christ, sharing his sufferings so as to share his glory."
                                        Romans 8:16-17

"My dear people, we are already the children of God but what we are to be in the future has not yet been revealed; all we know is, that when it is revealed we shall be like him because we shall see him as he really is."
                                        I John 3:2

Our Friend

"I shall not call you servants any more, because a servant does not know his master's business; I call you friends, because I have made known to you everything I have learned from my Father." **John 15:15**

"This is my commandment: love one another, as I have loved you. A man can have no greater love than to lay down his life for his friends. You are my friends, if you do what I command you." . **John 15:12-14**

"To you my friends I say: Do not be afraid of those who kill the body and after that can do no more." **Luke 12:4**

"Look, I am standing at the door, knocking. If one of you hears me calling and opens the door, I will come in to share his meal, side by side with him." **Revelation 3:20**

"Jesus replied: 'If anyone loves me he will keep my word, and my Father will love him, and we shall come to him and make our home with him.'" **John 14:23**

"Anybody who receives my commandments and keeps them will be one who loves me; and anybody who loves me will be loved by my Father, and I shall love him and show myself to him." **John 14:21**

"For where two or three meet in my name, I shall be there with them."   **Mattew 18:20**

"Because God by calling you has joined you to his Son, Jesus Christ; and God is faithful." **I Corinthians 1:9**

"What we have seen and heard we are telling you so that you too may be in union with us, as we are in union with the Father and with his Son Jesus Christ."
I John 1:3

Our Example

"This, in fact, is what you were called to do, because Christ suffered for you and left an example for you to follow the way he took."   **I Peter 2:21**

"Only when the one who claims to be living in him is living the same kind of life as Christ lived."
                                              I John 2:6

"Try, then, to imitate God, as children of his that he loves, and follow Christ by loving as he loved you, giving himself up in our place as a fragrant offering and a sacrifice to God."   **Ephesians 5:1-2**

"This is not to happen among you. No; anyone who wants to become great among you must be your servant, and anyone who wants to be first among you must be slave to all. For the Son of Man himself did not come to be served but to serve, and to give his life as a ransom for many."
                                              Mark 10:43-45

"If I, then, the Lord and Master, have washed your feet, you should wash each other's feet. I have given you an example so that you may copy what I have done to you."
                                              John 13:14-15

"I give you a new commandment: love one another; just as I have loved you, you also must love one another."
                                              John 13:34

"This has taught us love – that he gave up his life for us; and we, too, ought to give up our lives for our brothers."

I John 3:16

"And may he who helps us when we refuse to give up, help you all to be tolerant with each other, following the example of Christ Jesus, so that united in mind and voice you may give glory to the God and Father of our Lord Jesus Christ. It can only be to God's glory, then, for you to treat each other in the same friendly way as Christ treated you."

Romans 15:5-7

"Bear with one another; forgive each other as soon as a quarrel begins. The Lord has forgiven you; now you must do the same."

Colossians 3:13

Our Life

"All that came to be had life in him and that life was the light of men."
                              John 1:4

"Jesus said: 'I am the Way, the Truth and the Life. No one can come to the Father except through me.'"
                              John 14:6

"I tell you most solemnly, whoever listens to my words, and believes in the one who sent me, has eternal life; without being brought to judgment he has passed from death to life."
                              John 5:24

"And yet you refuse to come to me for life!"
                              John 5:40

"Yes, it is my Father's will that whoever sees the Son and believes in him shall have eternal life, and that I shall raise him up on the last day."   **John 6:40**

"I tell you most solemnly, everybody who believes has eternal life."
                              John 6:47

"Jesus replied: I tell you most solemnly, if you do not eat the flesh of the Son of Man and drink his blood, you will not have life in you. Anyone who does eat my flesh and drink my blood has eternal life, and I shall raise him up on the last day."
                              John 6:53-54

"As I, who am sent by the living Father, myself draw life from the Father, so whoever eats me will draw life from me."
John 6:57

"Simon Peter answered, 'Lord, who shall we go to? You have the message of eternal life.'" **John 6:68**

"The thief comes only to steal and kill and destroy. I have come so that they may have life and have it to the full."
John 10:10

"The sheep that belong to me listen to my voice; I know them and they follow me. I give them eternal life; they will never be lost and no one will ever steal them from me."
John 10:27-28

"Jesus said: 'I am the resurrection. If anyone believes in me, even though he dies he will live, and whoever lives and believes in me will never die. Do you believe this?'"
John 11:25-26

"There were many other signs that Jesus worked and the disciples saw, but they are not recorded in this book. These are recorded so that you may believe that Jesus is the Christ, the son of God, and that believing this you may have life through his name." **John 20:30-31**

"Let your thoughts be on heavenly things, not on the things that are on the earth, because you have died, and now the life you have is hidden with Christ in God. But when Christ is revealed – and he is your life – you too will be revealed in all your glory with him."

Colossians 3:2-4

"This is the testimony: God has given us eternal life and this life is in his Son; anyone who has the Son has life, anyone who does not have the Son does not have life."

I John 5:11-12

"I have written all this to you so that you who believe in the name of the Son of God may be sure that you have eternal life." **I John 5:13**

Our Everything

"In return my God will fulfill all your needs, in Christ Jesus, as lavishly as only God can." **Philippians 4:19**

"And there is no limit to the blessings which God can send you – he will make sure that you will always have all you need for yourselves in every possible circumstance, and still have something to spare for all sorts of good works."
II Corinthians 9:8

"Blessed be God the Father of our Lord Jesus Christ, who has blessed us with all the spiritual blessings of heaven in Christ." **Ephesians 1:3**

"I tell you therefore: everything you ask and pray for, believe that you have it already, and it will be yours."
Mark 11:24

"Whatever you ask for in my name I will do, so that the Father may be glorified in the Son."
John 14:13

"Ask, and it will be given to you; search, and you will find; knock, and the door will be opened to you. For the one who asks always receives; the one who searches always finds; the one who knocks will always have the door opened to him. " **Matthew 7:7-8**

"When that day comes, you will not ask me any questions. I tell you most solemnly, anything you ask for from the Father he will grant in my name. Until now you have not asked for anything in my name. Ask and you will receive, and so your joy will be complete." **John 16:23-24**

"And if you have faith, everything you ask for in prayer you will receive." **Mattew 21:22**

"If you remain in me and my words remain in you, you may ask what you will and you shall get it."
John 15:7

"In the one who is the head of every Sovereignty and Power." **Colossians 2:10**

"There is nothing I cannot master with the help of the One who gives me strength." **Philippians 4:13**

"And whatever we ask him, we shall receive, because we keep his commandments and live the kind of life that he wants." **I John 3:22**

"Jesus answered: 'I am the bread of life. He who comes to me will never be hungry; he who believes in me will never thirst.'" **John 6:35**

"Jesus replied: 'Whoever drinks this water will get thirsty again; but anyone who drinks the water that I shall give will never be thirsty again: the water that I shall give will turn into a spring inside him, welling up to eternal life.'"
John 4:13-14

"In forgiving all your offenses, in curing all your diseases, in redeeming your life from the Pit, in crowning you with love and tenderness, in filling your years with prosperity, in renewing your youth like an eagle's."

Psalms 103[102]:3-5

"Yahweh is my shepherd, I lack nothing."

Psalms 23[22]:1

"Since God did not spare his own Son, but gave him up to benefit us all, we may be certain, after such a gift, that he will not refuse anything he can give."

Romans 8:32

"By his divine power, he has given us all the things that we need for life and for true devotion, bringing us to know God himself, who has called us by his own glory and goodness. In making these gifts, he has given us the guarantee of something very great and wonderful to come: through them you will be able to share the divine nature and to escape corruption in a world that is sunk in vice."

II Peter 1:3-4

"We teach what scripture calls: the things that no eye has seen and no ear has heard, things beyond the mind of man, all that God has prepared for those who love him."

I Corinthians 2:9

4

Who is the Holy Spirit?

God

"In the beginning God created the heavens and the earth. Now the earth was a formless void, there was darkness over the deep, and God's spirit hovered over the water."

Genesis 1:1-2

"Didn't you realize that you were God's temple and that the Spirit of God was living among you?"

I Corinthians 3:16

"We teach what scripture calls: the things that no eye has seen and no ear has heard, things beyond the mind of man, all that God has prepared for those who love him. These are the very things that God has revealed to us through the Spirit, for the Spirit reaches the depths of everything, even the depths of God. After all, the depths of a man can only be known by his own spirit, not by any other man, and in the same way the depths of God can only be known by the Spirit of God." **I Corinthians 2:9-11**

"And you will know that I am Yahweh. [...] And I shall put my spirit in you, and you will live, and I shall resettle you on your own soil." **Ezequiel 37:13a.14a**

"After this I will pour out my spirit on all mankind. Your sons and daughters shall prophesy, your old men shall dream dreams, and your young men see visions." **Joel 3:1**

"I shall put my spirit in you, and make you keep my laws and sincerely respect my observances. You will live in the land which I gave your ancestors. You shall be my people and I will be your God." **Ezekiel 36:27-28**

"The spirit of the Lord Yahweh has been given to me, for Yahweh has anointed me. He has sent me to bring good news to the poor, to bind up hearts that are broken; to proclaim liberty to captives, freedom to those in prison." **Isaiah 61:1**

"Teach me to obey you, since you are my God; may your good spirit guide me on to level ground." **Psalms 143[142]:10**

"The spirit of Yahweh speaks through me, his word is on my tongue." **II Samuel 23:2**

"There is a variety of gifts but always the same Spirit; there are all sorts of service to be done, but always to the same Lord; working in all sorts of different ways in different people, it is the same God who is working in all of them."

I Corinthians 12:4-6

"We can know that we are living in him and he is living in us because he lets us share his Spirit."

I John 4:13

"In other words, anyone who objects is not objecting to a human authority, but to God, who gives you his Holy Spirit."

I Thessalonians 4:8

"'Ananias,' Peter said, 'how can Satan have so possessed you that you should lie to the Holy Spirit and keep back part of the money from the land? While you still owned the land, wasn't it yours to keep, and after you had sold it wasn't the money yours to do with as you liked? What put this scheme into your mind? It is not to men that you have lied, but to God.'"

Acts 5:3-4

Divine Strength*

"The Spirit too comes to help us in our weakness. For when we cannot choose words in order to pray properly, the Spirit himself expresses our plea in a way that could never be put into words, and God who knows everything in our hearts knows perfectly well what he means, and that the pleas of the saints expressed by the Spirit are according to the mind of God."   **Romans 8:26-27**

"But you will receive power when the Holy Spirit comes on you, and then you will be my witnesses not only in Jerusalem but throughout Judaea and Samaria, and indeed to the ends of the earth."   **Acts 1:8**

"After saying this he breathed on them and said: 'Receive the Holy Spirit.'"   **John 20:22**

"Jesus replied: 'I tell you most solemnly, unless a man is born through water and the Spirit, he cannot enter the kingdom of God.'"   **John 3:5**

"'The Holy Spirit will come upon you,' the angel answered, 'and the power of the Most High will cover you with its shadow.'"   **Luke 1:35a-b**

"Do not drug yourselves with wine; this is simply dissipation; be filled with the Spirit."   **Ephesians 5:18**

---

* Through the Word of God we acquire the knowledge that the Holy Spirit is not only the strength and power of God but is also the Person of God.

"It is for that reason that I want you to understand that on the one hand no one can be speaking under the influence of the Holy Spirit and say, 'Curse Jesus,' and on the other hand, no one can say, 'Jesus is Lord,' unless he is under the influence of the Holy Spirit." **I Corinthians 12:3**

"Filled with the Holy Spirit, Jesus left the Jordan and was led by the Spirit through the wilderness, being tempted there by the devil for forty days. During that time he ate nothing and at the end he was hungry."
Luke 4:1-2

"Jesus, with the power of the Spirit in him, returned to Galilee; and his reputation spread throughout the countryside." **Luke 4:14**

"God had anointed him with the Holy Spirit and with power, and because God was him, Jesus went about doing good and curing all who had fallen into the power of the devil." **Acts 10:38**

"They were infuriated when they heard this, and ground their teeth at him. But Stephen, filled with the Holy Spirit, gazed into heaven and saw the glory of God, and Jesus standing at God's right hand. 'I can see heaven thrown open,' he said, 'and the Son of Man standing at the right hand of God.'" **Acts 7:54-56**

"While Peter was still speaking the Holy Spirit came down on all the listeners. Jewish believers who had accompanied Peter were all astonished that the gift of the Holy Spirit should be poured out on the pagans too, since they could hear them speaking strange languages and proclaiming the greatness of God." **Acts10:44-46a**

"I had scarcely begun to speak when the Holy Spirit came down on them in the same way as it came on us at the beginning." **Acts 11:15**

"This, then, is what I pray, kneeling before the Father. [...] Out of his infinite glory, may he give you the power through his Spirit for your hidden self to grow strong." **Ephesians 3:14.16**

The Third Person of the Holy Trinity

"Everyone who says a word against the Son of Man will be forgiven, but he who blasphemes against the Holy Spirit will not be forgiven." **Luke 12:10**

"When they take you before synagogues and magistrates and authorities, do not worry about how to defend yourselves or what to say, because when the time comes, the Holy Spirit will teach you what you must say." **Luke 12:11-12**

"But the Advocate, the Holy Spirit, whom the Father will send in my name, will teach you everything and remind you of all I have said to you." **John 14:26**

"But when the Spirit of truth comes he will lead you to the complete truth, since he will not be speaking as from himself but will say only what he has learned; and he will tell you of the things to come. He will glorify me, since all he tells you will be taken from what is mine." **John 16:13-14**

"You stubborn people, with your pagan hearts and pagan ears. You are always resisting the Holy Spirit, just as your ancestors used to do." **Acts 7:51**

"The Spirit himself and our spirit bear united witness that we are children of God. And if we are children we are heirs as well: heirs of God and coheirs with Christ, sharing his sufferings so as to share his glory." **Romans 8:16-17**

"It was revealed to them that the news they brought of all the things which have now been announced to you, by those who preached to you the Good News through the Holy Spirit sent from heaven, was for you and not for themselves. Even the angels long to catch a glimpse of these things."
I Peter 1:12

"And you may be sure that anyone who tramples on the Son of God, and who treats the blood of the covenant which sanctified him as if it were not holy, and who insults the Spirit of grace, will be condemned to a far severer punishment." **Hebrews 10:29**

"By virtue of that one single offering, he has achieved the eternal perfection of all whom he is sanctifying. The Holy Spirit assures us of this." **Hebrews 10:14-15a**

"The Spirit has explicitly said that during the last times there will be some who will desert the faith and choose to listen to deceitful spirits and doctrines that come from the devils." **I Timothy 4:1**

"So that there are three witnesses, the Spirit, the water and the blood, and all three of them agree."
I John 5:7-8

"It has been decided by the Holy Spirit and by ourselves not to saddle you with any burden beyond these essentials: you are to abstain from food sacrificed to idols, from blood, from the meat of strangled animals and from fornication. Avoid these, and you will do what is right. Farewell."
Acts 15:28-29

"The Spirit and the Bride say, 'Come.' Let everyone who listens answer, 'Come.' Then let all who are thirsty come: all who want it may have the water of life, and have it free."
Revelation 22:17

"They were all filled with the Holy Spirit, and began to speak foreign languages as the Spirit gave them the gift of speech." **Acts 2:4**

"Otherwise you will only be grieving the Holy Spirit of God who has marked you with his peal for you to be set free when the day comes." **Ephesians 4:30**

"I shall ask the Father, and he will give you another Advocate to be with you for ever, that Spirit of truth whom the world can never receive since it neither sees nor knows him; but you know him, because he is with you, he is in you." **John 14:16-17**

"Go, therefore, make disciples of all the nations; baptize them in the name of the Father and of the Son and of the Holy Spirit." **Matthew 28:19**

"When he had been at table with them, he had told them not to leave Jerusalem, but to wait there for what the Father had promised. 'It is,' he had said, 'what you have heard me speak about: John baptized with water but you, not many days from now, will be baptized with the Holy Spirit.'" **Acts 1:4-5**

"As soon as Jesus was baptized he came up from the water, and suddenly the heavens opened and he saw the

Spirit of God descending like a dove and coming down on him. And a voice spoke from heaven, 'This is my Son, the Beloved; my favor rests on him.'"   **Matthew 3:16-17**

"Now you too, in him, have heard the message of the truth and the good news of your salvation, and have believed it; and you too have been stamped with the seal of the Holy Spirit of the Promise."   **Ephesians 1:13**

"If anyone has ears to hear, let him listen to what the Spirit is saying to the churches: those who prove victorious I will feed from the tree of life set in God's paradise."
Revelation 2:7

5

The Necessity of Salvation

"The fact is, I know of nothing good living in me – living, that is, in my unspiritual self – for though the will to do what is good is in me, the performance is not, with the result that instead of doing the good things I want to do, I carry out the sinful things I do not want. When I act against my will, then, it is not my true self doing it, but sin which lives in me."   **Romans 7:18-20**

"In my inmost self I dearly love God's Law, but I can see that my body follows a different law that battles against the law which my reason dictates. This is what makes me a prisoner of that law of sin which lives inside my body. What a wretched man I am! Who will rescue me from this body doomed to death?"   **Romans 7:22-24**

"Our sins and crimes weigh heavily on us; we are wasting away because of them."   **Ezekiel 33:10b**

"No, the hand of Yahweh is not too short to save, nor his ear too dull to hear. But your iniquities have made a gulf between you and your God." **Isaiah 59:1-2a**

"Happy the man whom Yahweh accuses of no guilt, whose spirit is incapable of deceit! All the time I kept silent, my bones were wasting away with groans, day in, day out; day and night your hand lay heavy on me; my heart grew parched as stubble in summer drought. At last I admitted to you I had sinned; no longer concealing my guilt, I said, 'I will go to Yahweh and confess my fault.' And you, you have forgiven the wrong I did, have pardoned my sin."

Psalms [32]31:2-5

"Yahweh, do not punish me in your rage, or reprove me in the heat of anger. Your arrows have pierced deep, your hand has pressed down on me; no soundness in my flesh now you are angry, no health in my bones, because of my sin. My guilt is overwhelming me, it is too heavy a burden."

Psalms 38[37]:1-4

"Have mercy on me, O God, in your goodness, in your great tenderness wipe away my faults; wash me clean of my guilt, purify me from my sin. For I am well aware of my faults, I have my sin constantly in mind, having sinned against none other than you, having done what you regard as wrong."

Psalms 51[50]:1-4a

"I pleaded with Yahweh my God and made this confession: 'O Lord, God great and to be feared, you keep the convenant and have kindness for those who love you and keep your commandments: we have sinned, we have done wrong, we have acted wickedly, we have betrayed your commandments and your ordinances and turned away from them. [...] And have not listened to the voice of Yahweh our God nor followed the laws he has given us through his servants the prophets." **Daniel 9:4-5.10**

"The anger of God is being revealed from heaven against all the impiety and depravity of men who keep truth imprisoned in their wickedness. [...] And so they are steeped in all sorts of depravity, rottenness, greed and malice, and addicted to envy, murder, wrangling, treachery and spite. Libelers, slanderers, enemies of God, rude, arrogant and boastful, enterprising in sin, rebellious to parents, without brains, honor, love or pity. They know what God's verdict is: that those who behave like this deserve to die – and yet they do it; and what is worse, encourage others to do the same." **Romans 1:18.29-32**

"Jesus answered: 'I tell you most solemnly, unless a man is born from above, he cannot see the kingdom of God.'" **John 3:3**

"Both Jew and pagan sinned and forfeited God's glory." **Romans 3:23**

"So in their case this prophecy of Isaiah is being fulfilled: You will listen and listen again, but not understand, see and see again, but not perceive. For the heart of this nation has grown coarse, their ears are dull of hearing, and they have shut their eyes, for fear they should see with their eyes, hear with their ears, understand with their heart, and be converted and be healed by me." **Matthew 13:14-15**

"For the wage paid by sin is death."

Romans 6:23a

"Your stubborn refusal to repent is only adding to the anger God will have toward you on that day of anger when his just judgments will be made known. He will repay each one as his works deserve." **Romans 2:5-6**

"It is death to limit oneself to what is unspiritual; life and peace can only come with concern for the spiritual. That is because to limit oneself to what is unspiritual is to be at enmity with God: such a limitation never could and never does submit to God's law. People who are interested only in unspiritual things can never be pleasing to God."

Romans 8:6-8

"There is a way that some think right, but it leads in the end to death." **Proverbs 14:12**

"I have told you often, and I repeat it today with tears, there are many who are behaving as the enemies of the cross of Christ. They are destined to be lost. They make foods into their god and they are proudest of something they ought to think shameful; the things they think important are earthly things." **Philippians 3:18-19**

"Whoever makes thanksgiving his sacrifice honors me; to the upright man I will show how God can save."

Psalms 50[49]:23

"May God show kindness and bless us, and make his face smile on us! For then the earth will acknowledge your ways and all the nations will know of your power to save."

Psalms 67[66]:1-2

"You will never save the wicked, if they do not study your statutes."   **Psalms 119[118]:155**

"See now, he is the God of my salvation I have trust now and no fear, for Yahweh is my strength, my song, he is my salvation."   **Isaiah 12:2**

"God overlooked that sort of thing when men were ignorant, but now he is telling everyone everywhere that they must repent."   **Acts 17:30**

6

Promises of God for Our Salvation

"You yourselves are my witnesses – it is Yahweh who speaks – my servants whom I have chosen, that men may know and believe me and understand that it is I. No god was formed before me, nor will be after me. I, I am Yahweh, there is no other savior but me."   **Isaiah 43:10-11**

"Then all mankind shall know that I, Yahweh, am your savior and that your redeemer is the Mighty One of Jacob."
Isaiah 49:26b

"And you shall now that I, Yahweh, am your savior, that your redeemer is the Mighty One of Jacob."
Isaiah 60:16b

"This Yahweh proclaims to the ends of the earth: Say to the daughter of Zion, 'Look, your savior comes, the prize of

his victory with him, his trophies before him.' They shall be called 'The Holy People,' 'Yahweh's Redeemed.' And you shall be called 'The-sought-after,' 'City-not-forsaken'."
Isaiah 62:11,12

"For he that casts down the boasting of the braggart is he that saves the man of downcast eyes. If a man is innocent, he will bring him freedom, and freedom for you if your hands are kept unstained." **Job 22:29-30**

"God is the shield that protects me, he preserves upright hearts." **Psalms 7:11**

"I was pressed, pressed, about to fall, but Yahweh came to my help; Yahweh is my strength and may song, he has been my savior." **Psalms 118[117]:13-14**

"Righteous in all that he does, Yahweh acts only out of love, standing close to all who invoke him, close to all who invoke Yahweh faithfully. Those who fear him need only to ask to be answered; he hears their cries for help and saves them. Under his protection the pious are safe."
Psalms 145[144]:17-20a

"The Lord Yahweh will wipe away the tears from every cheek; he will take away his people's shame everywhere on earth, for Yahweh has said so. Tha day, it will be said: See, this is our God in whom we hoped for salvation; Yahweh is the one in whom we hoped. We exult and we rejoice that he has saved us." **Isaiah 25:8b-9**

"Say to them, 'as I live it is the Lord Yahweh who speaks – I take pleasure, not in the death of a wicked man, but in the turning back of a wicked man who changes his ways to win life. Come back, come back from your evil ways. Why are you so anxious to die, House of Israel?'"

Ezekiel 33:11

"When that day comes, word will come to Jerusalem: Zion, have no fear, do not let your hands fall limp. Yahweh your God is in your midst, a victorious warrior. He will exult with joy over you, he will renew you by his love; he will dance with shouts of joy for you." **Zephaniah 3:16-17**

"Now I am going to save my people [...]. I will bring them back to live inside Jerusalem. They shall be my people and I will be their God in faithfulness and integrity. [...] For I mean to spread peace everywhere; the vine will give its fruit, the earth its increase, and heaven its dew. I am going to bestow all these blessings on the remnant of this people."

Zechariah 8:7b.8.12

"She will give birth to a son and you must name him Jesus, because he is the one who is to save his people from their sins." **Matthew 1:21**

"If anyone wants to be a follower of mine, let him renounce himself and take up his cross and follow me. For anyone who wants to save his life will lose it; but anyone who loses his life for my sake will find it. [...] 'For the Son of Man is going to come in the glory of his Father with his angels, and, when he does, he will reward each one according to his behavior.'" **Matthew 16:24b-25.27**

"You will be hated by all men on account of my name; but the man who stands firm to the end will be saved."

Mark 13:13

"For the Son of Man has come to seek out and save what was lost." **Luke 19:10**

"As Moses lifted up the serpent in the desert, so that everyone who believes may have eternal life in him." **John 3:14-15**

"Yes, God loved the world so much that he gave his only Son, so that everyone who believes in him may not be lost but may have eternal life. For God sent his Son into the world not to condemn the world, but so that through him the world might be saved." **John 3:16-17**

"But what proves that God loves us is that Christ died for us while we were still sinners. Having died to make us righteous, is it likely that he would now fail to save us from God's anger?" **Romans 5:8-9**

"By his own right hand God has now raised him up to be leader and savior, to give repentance and forgiveness of sins through him to Israel." **Acts 5:31**

"To keep his promise, God has raised up for Israel one of David's descendants. Jesus, as Savior. [...] It is to us, their children, that he has fulfilled it, by raising Jesus from the dead. [...] My brothers, I want you to realize that it is through him that forgiveness of your sins is proclaimed." **Acts 13:23.33a.38a**

"Become a believer in the Lord Jesus, and you will be saved, and your household too." **Acts 16:31b**

"When we were reconciled to God by the death of his Son, we were still enemies; now that we have been reconciled, surely we may count on being saved by the life of his Son?"
Romans 5:10

"In whom, through his blood, we gain our freedom, the forgiveness of our sins. Such is the richness of the grace which he has showered on us in all wisdom and insight."
Ephesians 1:7-8

"So I bear it all for the sake of those who are chosen, so that in the end they may have the salvation that is in Christ Jesus and the eternal glory that comes with it. Here is a saying that you can rely on: If we have died with him, then we shall live with him. If we hold firm, then we shall reign with him."
II Timothy 2:10-12a

"For of all the names in the world given to men, this is the only one by which we can be saved."
Acts 4:12

Part II

1

Promises of God for Your Life

In Situations of:

Discouragement

"Be strong, stand firm, have no fear of them, no terror, for Yahweh your God is going with you; he will not fail you or desert you."   **Deuteronomy 31:6**

"Yahweh is my light and my salvation, whom need I fear? Yahweh is the fortress of my life, of whom should I be afraid? [...] This I believe: I shall see the goodness of Yahweh, in the land of the living. Put your hope in Yahweh, be strong, let your heart be bold, put your hope in Yahweh."
                              Psalms 27[26]:1.13-14

"The wicked man spies on the virtuous, seeking to kill him; Yahweh will never leave him in those clutches, or let him be condemned under trial." **Psalms 37[36]:32-33**

"Or who ever feared him steadfastly and was left forsaken? Or who ever called out to him, and was ignored?"
Ecclesiasticus 2:12

"Consider, then, how in generation after generation all who hope in him will not be found to falter."
I Maccabees 2:61

"Another man is a poor creature begging for assistance, badly off for support, but rich in poverty, and the Lord turns a favorable eye on him, sets him on his feet out of his abject condition, and enables him to hold his head high, to the utter amazement of many." **Ecclesiasticus 11:12-13**

"The patient man will hold out till the time comes, but his joy will break out in the end."
Ecclesiasticus 1:29

"Young men may grow tired and weary, youths may stumble, but those who hope in Yahweh renew their strength, they put out wings like eagles. They run and do not grow weary, walk and never tire." **Isaiah 40:30-31**

"We are in difficulties on all sides, but never cornered; we see no answer to our problems, but never despair; we have been persecuted, but never deserted; knocked down, but never killed; always, wherever we may be, we carry with us in our body the death of Jesus, so that the life of Jesus, too, may always be seen in our body." **II Corinthians 4:8-10**

"Meanwhile, let us go forward on the road that has brought us to where we are." **Philippians 3:16**

"Take care, brothers, that there is not in any one of your community a wicked mind, so unbelieving as to turn away from the living God. Every day, as long as this 'today' lasts, keep encouraging one another so that none of you is hardened by the lure of sin, because we shall remain co-heirs with Christ only if we keep a grasp on our first confidence right to the end." **Hebrews 3:12-14**

"We must never get tired of doing good because if we dont't give up the struggle we shall get our harvest at the proper time." **Galatians 6:9**

"Be as confident now, then, since the reward is so great. You will need endurance to do God's will and gain what he has promised." **Hebrews 10:35-36**

"Believe me, God neither spurns a stainless man, nor lends his aid to the evil. Once again your cheeks will fill with laughter, from your lips will break a cry of joy." **Job 8:20-21**

"Though I live surrounded by trouble, you keep me alive – to my enemies' fury! You stretch your hand out and save me." **Psalms 138[137]:7**

"You, Israel, my servant [...]; you to whom I said, 'You are my servant, I have chosen you, not rejected you,' do not be afraid, for I am with you; stop being anxious and watchful, for I am your God. I give you strength, I bring you help, I uphold you with my victorious right hand."

Isaiah 41:8a.9b-10

"Here is my servant whom I uphold, my chosen one in whom my soul delights. I have endowed him with my spirit. [...] I, Yahweh, have called you to serve the cause of right; I have taken you by the hand and formed you."

Isaiah 42:1a-b.6a-b

"Let us not lose sight of Jesus, who leads us in our faith and brings it to perfection." **Hebrews 12:1b**

"Though this outer man of ours may be falling into decay, the inner man is renewed day by day. Yes, the troubles which are soon over, though they weigh little, train us for the carrying of a weight of eternal glory which is out of all proportion to them." **II Corinthians 4:16b-17**

"Think of the way he stood such opposition from sinners and then you will not give up for want of courage."

Hebrews 12:3

"Have you forgotten that encouraging text in which you are addressed as sons? My son, when the Lord corrects you, do not treat it lightly; but do not get discouraged when he reprimands you. For the Lord trains the ones that he loves and he punishes all those that he acknowledges as his sons. Suffering is part of your training; God is treating you as his sons. Has there ever been any son whose father did not train him?" **Hebrews 12:5-7**

In Situations of:

Concern

"That is why I am telling you not to worry about your life and what you are to eat, nor about your body and how you are to clothe it. Surely life means more than food, and the body more than clothing! Look at the birds in the sky. They do not sow or reap or gather into barns; yet your heavenly Father feeds them. Are you not worth much more than they are?"   **Matthew 6:25-26**

"Can any of you, for all his worrying, add one single cubit to his span of life? And why worry about clothing? Think of the flowers growing in the fields; they never have to work or spin; yet I assure you that not even Solomon in all his regalia was robed like one of these. Now if that is how God clothes the grass in the field which is there today and thrown into the furnace tomorrow, will he not much more look after you, you men of little faith?"   **Matthew 6:27-30**

"So do not worry; do not say, 'What are we to eat? What are we to drink? How are we to be clothed?' It is the pagans who set their hearts on all these things. Your heavenly Father knows you need them all. Set your hearts on his kingdom first, and on his righteousness, and all these other things will be given you as well. So do not worry about tomorrow: tomorrow will take care of itself. Each day has enough trouble of its own."   **Mattew 6:31-34**

"There is no need to worry; but if there is anything you need, pray for it, asking God for it with prayer and thanksgiving, and that peace of God, which is so much greater than we can understand, will guard your hearts and your thoughts, in Christ Jesus." **Philippians 4:6-7**

"In return my God will fulfill all your needs, in Christ Jesus, as lavishly as only God can." **Philippians 4:19**

"Do not let your hearts be troubled. Trust in God still, and trust in me." **John 14:1**

"Unload all your worries on to him, since he is looking after you." **I Peter 5:7**

"In peace I lie down, and fall asleep at once, since you alone, Yahweh, make me rest secure."
Psalms 4:8

"When they take you before synagogues and magistrates, and authorities, do not worry about how to defend yourselves or what to say, because when the time comes, the Holy Spirit will teach you what you must say." **Luke 12:11-12**

"For my part, I look to Yahweh, my hope is in the God who will save me; my God will hear me."
Micah 7:7

"I lift my eyes to the mountains: where is help to come from? Help comes to me from Yahweh, who made heaven and earth." **Psalms 121[120]:1-2**

"I am the vine, you are the branches. Whoever remains in me, with me in him, bears fruit in plenty; for cut off from me you can do nothing." **John 15:5**

In Situations of:

Anguish and Depression

"Do not be afraid, for I am with you; stop being anxious and watchful, for I am your God. I give you strength, I bring you help, I uphold you with my victorious right hand."
Isaiah 41:10

"I will not leave you orphans; I will come back to you."
John 14:18

"But now, thus says Yahweh, who created you: [...] Should you pass through the sea, I will be with you; or through rivers, they will not swallow you up. Should you walk through fire, you will not be scorched and the flames will not burn you Because you are precious in my eyes, because you are honored and I love you. [...] Do not be afraid, for I am with you."
Isaiah 43:1a.2.4a.5a

"Does a woman forget her baby at the breast, or fail to cherish the son of her womb? Yet even if these forget, I will never forget you. See, I have branded you on the palms of my hands."
Isaiah 49:15-16a

"The angel of Yahweh pitches camp around those who fear him; and he keeps them safe. How good Yahweh is – only taste and see! Happy the man who takes shelter in him. Fear Yahweh, you his holy ones: those who fear him want for nothing."
Psalms 34[33]:7-9

119

"My dear people, you must not think it unaccountable that you should be tested by fire. There is nothing extraordinary in what has happened to you. If you can have some share in the sufferings of Christ, be glad, because you will enjoy a much greater gladness when his glory is revealed. It is a blessing for you when they insult your for bearing the name of Christ, because it means that you have the Spirit of glory, the Spirit of God resting on you."

I Peter 4:12-14

"He is going to judge the world with justice, and pronounce a true verdict on the nations."

Psalms 9:8

"Turn your ear to me, make haste! Be a sheltering rock for me, a walled fortress to save me! [...] Pull me out of the net they have spread for me, for you are my refuge. [...] I will exult, and rejoice in your love! You, who have seen my wretchedness, and known the miseries of my soul."

Psalms 31[30]:3.5.8

"I seek Yahweh, and he answers me and frees me from all my fears. Every face turned to him grows brighter and is never ashamed. A cry goes up from the poor man, and Yahweh hears, and helps him in all his troubles."

Psalms 34[33]:4-6

"They cry for help and Yahweh hears and rescues them from all their troubles."   **Psalms 34[33]:17**

"That is why each of your servants prays to you in time of trouble; even if floods come rushing down, they will never reach him. You are a hiding place for me, you guard me when in trouble, you surround me with songs of deliverance."

Psalms 32[31]:6-7

"But you will seek Yahweh your God from there, and if you seek him with all your heart and with all your soul, you shall find him."

Deuteronomy 4:29

"In my distress I called to Yahweh and to my God I cried; from his Temple he heard my voice, my cry came to his ears."

II Samuel 22:7

"My eyes are always on Yahweh, for he releases my feet from the net. Turn to me, take pity on me, alone and wretched as I am! Relieve the distress of my heart, free me from my sufferings."

Psalms [25]24:15-17

"And in the middle of all my troubles you console me and make me happy."

Psalms 94[93]:19

"Play music in Yahweh's honor, you devout, remember his holiness, and praise him. His anger lasts a moment, his favor a lifetime; in the evening, a spell of tears, in the morning, shouts of joy."

Psalms 30[29]:4-5

"The Spirit too comes to help us in our weakness. For when we cannot choose words in order to pray properly, the Spirit himself expresses our plea in a way that could never be put into words, and God who knows everything in our hearts knows perfectly well what he means, and that the pleas of the saints expressed by the Spirit are according to the mind of God."

Romans 8:26-27

121

"A blessing on the man who puts his trust in Yahweh, with Yahweh for his hope. He is like a tree by the waterside that thrusts its roots to the stream: when the heat comes it feels no alarm, its foliage stays green; it has no worries in a year of drought, and never ceases to bear fruit."

Jeremiah 17:7-8

"God himself has said: I will not fail you or desert you, and so we can say with confidence: With the Lord to help me, I fear nothing: what can man do to me?"

Hebrews 13:5b-6

In Situations of:

Temptation

"Happy the man who stands firm when trials come. He has proved himself, and will win the prize of life, the crown that the Lord has promised to those who love him."

James 1:12

"The trials that you have had to bear are no more than people normally have. You can trust God not to let you be tried beyond your strength, and with any trial he will give you a way out of it and the strength to bear it."

I Corinthians 10:13

"Give in to God, then; resist the devil, and he will run away from you. The nearer you go to God, the nearer he will come to you. Clean your hands, you sinners, and clear your minds, you waverers. Look at your wretched condition, and weep for it in misery; be miserable instead of laughing, gloomy instead of happy. Humble yourselves before the Lord and he will lift you up."   **James 4:7-10**

"Be calm but vigilant, because your enemy the devil is prowling around like a roaring lion, looking for someone to eat. Stand up to him, strong in faith and in the knowledge that your brothers all over the world are suffering the same things. You will have to suffer only for a little while: the God of all grace who called you to eternal glory in Christ will see that all is well again: he will confirm, strengthen and support you."   **I Peter 5:8-10**

"Because anyone who has been begotten by God has already overcome the world; this is the victory over the world – our faith. Who can overcome the world? Only the man who believes that Jesus is the Son of God."

I John 5:4b-5

"Finally, grow strong in the Lord, with the strength of his power. Put God's armor on so as to be able to resist the devil's tactics. For it is not against human enemies that we have to struggle, but against the Sovereignties and the Powers who originate the darkness in this world, the spiritual army of evil in the heavens." **Ephesians 6:10-12**

"That is why you must not let sin reign in your mortal bodies or command your obedience to bodily passions, why you must not let any part of your body turn into an unholy weapon fighting on the side of sin; you should, instead, offer yourselves to God, and consider yourselves dead men brought back to life; you should make every part of your body into a weapon fighting on the side of God; and then sin will no longer dominate your life, since you are living by grace and not by law." **Romans 6:12-14**

"I only hope that you are also wise in what is good and innocent of what is bad. The God of peace will soon crush satan beneath your feet." **Romans 16:19b-20a**

"Take care, brothers, that there is not in any one of your community a wicked mind, so unbelieving as to turn away from the living God. Every day, as long as this 'today' last, keep encouraging one another so that none of you is hardened by the lure of sin, because we shall remain coheirs with Christ only if we keep a grasp on our first confidence right to the end." **Hebrews 3:12-14**

"These are all examples of how the Lord can rescue the good from the ordeal, and hold the wicked for their punishment until the day of Judgment."
II Peter 2:9

"These are the trials through which we triumph, by the power of him who loved us." **Romans 8:37**

In Situations of:

Financial Necessity

"So do not worry; do not say, 'What are we to eat? What are we to drink? How are we to be clothed?' It is the pagans who set their hearts on all these things. Your heavenly Father knows you need them all. Set your hearts on his kingdom first, and on his righteousness, and all these other things will be given you as well." **Matthew 6:31-33**

"All the blessings that follow shall come up with you and overtake you if only you obey the voice of Yahweh your God. You will be blessed in the town and blessed in the country. Blessed will be the fruit of your body, the produce of your soil, the issue of your livestock, the increase of your cattle, the young of your flock. Blessed will be your pannier and your bread bin. Blessed will you be coming in, and blessed going out. [...] Yahweh will summon a blessing for you in your barns and in all your undertakings, and will bless you in the land that Yahweh is giving you."

Deuteronomy 28:2-6.8

"Yahweh will give you great store of good things, the fruit of your body, the fruit of your cattle and the produce of your soil, in the land he swore to your fathers he would give you. Yahweh will open the heavens to you, his rich treasure house, to give you seasonable rain for your land and to bless all the work of your hands. You will make many nations your subjects, yet you will be subject to none. Yahweh will put you at the head, not at the tail; you will always be on

Top and never underneath, if you obey the commandments of Yahweh your God that I enjoin on you today, keeping and observing them." **Deuteronomy 28:11-13**

"Bring the full tithes and dues to the storehouse so that there may be food in my house, and then see if I do not open the floodgates of heaven for you and pour out blessing for you in abundance." **Malachi 3:10**

"In return my God will fulfill all your needs, in Christ Jesus, as lavishly as only God can." **Philippians 4:19**

"Have the book of this Law always on your lips; meditate on it day and night, so that you may carefully keep everything that is written in it. Then you will prosper in your dealings, then you will have success." **Joshua 1:8**

"Do not forget: thin sowing means thin reaping; the more you sow, the more you reap. Each one should give what he has decided in his own mind, not grudgingly or because he is made to, for God loves loves a cheerful giver. And there is no limit to the blessings which God can send you – he will make sure that you will always have all you need for yourselves in every possible circumstance, and still have something to spare for all sorts of good works."
II Corinthians 9:6-8

"Honor Yahweh with what goods you have and with the first fruits of all your returns; then your barns will be filled with wheat, your vats overflowing with new wine."
Proverbs 3:9-10

"Yahweh takes care of good men's lives, and their heritage will last for ever; they will not be at a loss when bad times come, in time of famine they will have more than they need." **Psalms 37[36]:18-19**

"Fear Yahweh, you his holy ones: those who fear him want for nothing. The young lion may go empty and hungry, but those who seek Yahweh lack nothing good."
Psalms 34[33]:9-10

"Commend what you do to Yahweh, and your plans will find achievement." **Proverbs 16:3**

"But see how the eye of Yahweh is on those who fear him, on those who rely on his love, to rescue their souls from death and keep them alive in famine."
Psalms 33[32]:18-19

"Put greed out of your lives and be content with whatever you have; God himself has said: I will not fail you or desert you." **Hebrews 13:5**

"The good man bequeaths his heritage to his children's children, the wealth of the sinner is stored up for the virtuous." **Proverbs 13:22**

"Warn those who are rich in this world's goods that they are not to look down on other people; and not to set their hopes on money, which is untrustworthy, but on God who, out of his riches, gives us all that we need for our happiness." **I Timothy 6:17**

"Now I am old, but ever since my youth I never saw a virtuous man deserted. [...] For Yahweh loves what is right, and never deserts the devout."   **Psalms 37[36]:25.28a**

"Yahweh is my shepherd, I lack nothing."
Psalms 23[22]:1

"Give, and there will be gifts for you: a full measure, pressed down, shaken together, and running over, will be poured into your lap; because the amount you measure out is the amount you will be given back."
Luke 6:38

In Situations of:

Frustration

"Do not be afraid, for I am with you; stop being anxious and watchful, for I am your God. I give you strength, I bring you help, I uphold you with my victorius right hand."
Isaiah 41:10

"There is no need to worry; but if there is anything you need, pray for it, asking God for it with prayer and thanksgiving, and that peace of God, which is so much greater than we can understand, will guard your hearts and your thoughts, in Christ Jesus." **Philippians 4:6-7**

"The Lord Yahweh comes to my help, so that I am untouched by the insults. So, too, I set my face like flint; I know I shall not be shamed. My vindicator is here at hand."
Isaiah 50:7-8a

"With God on our side who can be against us? Since God did not spare his own Son, but gave him up to benefit us all, we may be certain, after such a gift, that he will not refuse anything he can give." **Romans 8:31b-32**

"Yahweh thwarts the plans of nations, frustrates the intentions of peoples; but Yahweh's plans hold good for ever, the intentions of his heart from age to age."
Psalms 33[32]:10-11

"The eyes of the Lord watch over those who love him, he is their powerful protection and their strong support, their screen from the desert wind, their shelter from the midday sun, a guard against stumbling, an assurance against a fall. He revives the spirit and brightens the eyes, he gives healing, life and blessing." **Ecclesiasticus 34:19-20**

"This is why I am reminding you now to fan into a flame the gift that God gave you when I laid my hands on you. God's gift was not a spirit of timidity, but the Spirit of power and love and self-control." **II Timothy 1:6-7**

"Trust in Yahweh for ever, for Yahweh is the everlasting Rock." **Isaiah 26:4**

"Give in to God, then. [...] The nearer you go to God, the nearer he will come to you. [...] Humble yourselves before the Lord and he will lift you up."
James 4:7a.8a.10

"Trust wholeheartedly in Yahweh, put no faith in your own perception; in every course you take, have him in mind: he will see that your paths are smooth."
Proverbs 3:5-6

"My brothers, you will always have your trials but, when they come, try to treat them as a happy privilege [...]. He has proved himself, and will win the prize of life, the crown that the Lord has promised to those who love him."
James 1:2.12b

"Yahweh is an everlasting God. [...] He gives strength to the wearied, he strengthens the powerless. [...] those who hope in Yahweh renew their strength."

Isaiah 40:28b.29.31a

"We are quite confident that if we ask him for anything, and it is in accordance with his will, he will hear us; and, knowing that whatever we may ask, he hears us, we know that we have already been granted what we asked of him."

I John 5:14-15

Abandonment and Loneliness

"May Yahweh be a stronghold for the oppressed, a stronghold when times are hard. Those who acknowledge your name can rely on you, you never desert those who seek you, Yahweh." **Psalms 9:9-10**

"For Yahweh has not abandoned or deserted his hereditary people. And in the middle of all my troubles you console me and make me happy." **Psalms 94[93]:14.19**

"You are my help. Never leave me, never desert me, God, my savior! If my father and mother desert me, Yahweh will care for me still." **Psalms 27[26]:9b-10**

"We have been persecuted, but never deserted; knocked down, but never killed." **II Corinthians 4:9**

"Commit your fate to Yahweh, trust in him and he will act: making your virtue clear as the light, your integrity as bright as noon." **Psalms 37[36]:5-6**

"I rescue all who cling to me, I protect whoever knows my name, I answer everyone who invokes me, I am with them when they are in trouble; I bring them safety and honor." **Psalms 91[90]:14-15**

"God himself has said: I will not fail you or desert you, and so we can say with confidence: With the Lord to help me, I fear nothing: what can man do to me?"
Hebrews 13:5b-6

"The angel of Yahweh pitches camp around those who fear him; and he keeps them safe. How good Yahweh is – only taste and see! Happy the man who takes shelter in him."
Psalms 34[33]:7-8

"Look at the generations of old and see: who ever trusted in the Lord and was put to shame? Or who ever feared him steadfastly and was left forsaken? Or who ever called out to him, and was ignored?" **Ecclesiasticus 2:11-12**

"With Yahweh on my side, I fear nothing: what can man do to me? With Yahweh on my side, best help of all, I can triumph over my enemies." **Psalms 118[117]:6-7**

"Be strong, stand firm, have no fear of them, no terror, for Yahweh your God is going with you; he will not fail you or desert you." **Deuteronomy 31:6**

"But you will seek Yahweh your God from there, and if you seek him with all your heart and with all your soul, you shall find him. [...] For Yahweh your God is a merciful God and will not desert or destroy you or forget the covenant he made on oath with your fathers." **Deuteronomy 4:29.31**

"Father of orphans, defender of widows, such is God in his holy dwelling; God gives the lonely a permanent home, makes prisoners happy by setting them free, but rebels must live in an arid land." **Psalms 68[67]:5-6**

"I will not leave you orphans; I will come back to you."
John 14:18

"For the mountaions may depart, the hills be shaken, but my love for you will never leave you and my covenant of peace with you will never be shaken, says Yahweh who takes pity on you." **Isaiah 54:10**

"The poor and needy ask for water, and there is none, their tongue is parched with thirst. I, Yahweh, will answer them, I, the God of Israel, will not abandon them."
Isaiah 41:17

"For Zion was saying, 'Yahweh has abandoned me, the Lord has forgotten me.' Does a woman forget her baby at the breast, or fail to cherist the son of her womb? Yet even if these forget, I will never forget you. See, I have branded you on the palms of my bands." **Isaiah 49:14-16a**

"Since for the sake of his great name Yahweh will not desert his people, for it has pleased Yahweh to make you his people." **I Samuel 12:22**

"And know that I am with you always; yes, to the end of time." **Matthew 28:20b**

In Situations of:

Despondency

"Why so downcast, my soul, why do you sigh within me? Put your hope in God: I shall praise him yet, my savior, my God." **Psalms 42[41]:5-6a**

"For thus speaks the Most High, whose home is in eternity, whose name is holy: 'I live in a high and holy place, but I am also with the contrite and humbled spirit, to give the humbled spirit new life, to revive contrite hearts.'" **Isaiah 57:15**

"Yahweh is near to the brokenhearted, he helps those whose spirit is crushed." **Psalms 34[33]:18**

"Hard pressed, I invoked Yahweh, he heard me and came to my relief. [...] I would rather take refuge in Yahweh than rely on men; I would rather take refuge in Yahweh than rely on princes." **Psalms 118[117]:5.8-9**

"All of this was made by my hand and all of this is mine – it is Yahweh who speaks. But my eyes are drawn to the man of humbled and contrite spirit, who trembles at my word." **Isaiah 66:2**

"In God alone there is rest for my soul, from comes my safety; with him alone for my rock, my safety, my fortress, I can never fall." **Psalms 62[61]:1-2**

"Give thanks to Yahweh, for he is good. [...] He remembered us when we were down, his love is everlasting!"
Psalms 136[135]:1a.23

"Put your hope in Yahweh, be strong, let your heart be bold, put your hope in Yahweh." **Psalms 27[26]:14**

"But now, thus says Yahweh, who created you, Jacob, who formed you, Israel: Do not be afraid, for I have redeemed you; I have called you by your name, you are mine. [...] Because you are precious in my eyes, because you are honored and I love you. I give men in exchange for you, peoples in return for your life. Do not be afraid, for I am with you." **Isaiah 43:1.4-5a**

"You whom I brought from the confines of the earth and called from the ends of the world; you to whom I said, You are my servant, I have chosen you, not rejected you,' do not be afraid, for I am with you; stop being anxious and watchful, for I am your God. I give you strength, I bring you help, I uphold you with my victorious right hand." **Isaiah 41:9-10**

"I was pressed, pressed, about to fall, but Yahweh came to my help; Yahweh is my strength and my song, he has been my savior. [...] No, I shall not die, I shall live to recite the deeds of Yahweh." **Psalms 118[117]:13-14.17**

"There is nothing I cannot master with the help of the One who gives me strength." **Philippians 4:13**

"But those who hope in Yahweh renew their strength, they put out wings like eagles. They run and do not grow weary, walk and never tire." **Isaiah 40:31**

"That is why there is no weakening on our part, and instead, though this outer man of ours may be falling into decay, the inner man is renewed day by day. Yes, the troubles which are soon over, though they weigh little, train us for the carrying of a weight of eternal glory which is out of all proportion to them. And so we have no eyes for things that are visible, but only for things that are invisible; for visible things last only for a time, and the invisible things are eternal." **II Corinthians 4:16-18**

In Situations of:

Defeat

"He is to be praised; on Yahweh I call and am saved from my enemies."   **Psalms 18[17]:3**

"I rescue all who cling to me, I protect whoever knows my name, I answer everyone who invokes me, I am with them when they are in trouble; I bring them safety and honor."
                    Psalms 91[90]:14-15

"If you live in the shelter of Elyon and make your home in the shadow of Shaddai, you can say to Yahweh, 'My refuge, my fortress, my God in whom I trust!' He rescues you from the snares of fowlers hoping to destroy you; he covers you with his feathers, and you find shelter underneath his wings."
                    Psalms 91[90]:1-4

"In my distress I called to Yahweh and to my God I cried; from his Temple he heard my voice, my cry came to his ears. [...]He sends from on high and takes me, he draws me from deep waters, he delivers me from my powerful enemy, from a foe too strong for me. They assailed me on my day of disaster, but Yahweh was my support; he freed me, set me at large, he rescued me, since he loves me."
                    Psalms 18[17]:6.16-19

"But joy for all who take shelter in you, endless shouts of joy! Since you protect them, they exult in you, those who love your name."   **Psalms 5:11**

"There is no need to worry; [...] and that peace of God, which is so much greater than we can understand, will guard your hearts and your thoughts, in Christ Jesus."

Philippians 4:6a.7

"He will light up all that is hidden in the dark and reveal the secret intentions of men's hearts. Then will be the time for each one to have whatever praise he deserves from God." **I Corinthians 4:5b**

"After saying this, what can we add? With God on our side who can be against us? Since God did not spare his own Son, but gave him up to benefit us all, we may be certain, after such a gift, that he will not refuse anything he can give. Could anyone accuse those that God has chosen? When God acquits, could anyone condemn? Could Christ Jesus? No! He not only died for us – he rose from the dead, and there at God's right hand he stands and pleads for us." **Romans 8:31-34**

"But see how the eye of Yahweh is on those who fear him, on those who rely on his love, to rescue their souls from death and keep them alive in famine."

Psalms 33[32]:18-19

"Then you can invoke me in your troubles and I will rescue you, and you shall honor me." **Psalms 50[49]:15**

"Who rescues me from my ranging enemies. You lift me high above those who attack me, you deliver me from the man of violence. For this I will praise you, Yahweh, among the heathen and sing praise to your name."

Psalms 18[17]:48-49

"Yahweh guides a man's steps, they are sure, and he takes pleasure in his progress; he may fall, but never fatally, since Yahweh supports him by the hand."

Psalms 37[36]:23-24

"The eyes of the Lord watch over those who love him, he is their powerful protection and their strong support, their screen from the desert wind, their shelter from the midday sun, a guard against stumbling, an assurance against a fall. He revives the spirit and brightens the eyes, he gives healing life and blessing." **Ecclesiasticus 34:19-20**

"I was pressed, pressed, about to fall, but Yahweh came to my help; Yahweh is my strength and my song, he has been my savior." **Psalms 118[117]:13-14**

"I, for myself, appeal to God and Yahweh saves me; evening, morning, noon, I complain, I groan; he will hear me calling." **Psalms 55[54]:16-17**

"So let us thank God for giving us the victory through our Lord Jesus Christ." **I Corinthians 15:57**

"Because anyone who has been begotten by God has already overcome the world; this is the victory over the world – our faith." **I John 5:4b-c**

"Nothing therefore can come between us and the love of Christ, even if we are troubled or worried, or being persecuted, or lacking food or clothes, or being threatened or even attacked. Daily and reckoned as sheep for the slaughter. These are the trials through which we triumph, by the power of him who loved us." **Romans 8:35-37**

"I have told you all this so that you may find peace in me. In the world you will have trouble, but be brave: I have conquered the world."   **John 16:33**

"God is our shelter, our strength, ever ready to help in time of trouble."   **Psalms 46[45]:1**

"Yahweh thwarts the plans of nations, frustrates the intentions of peoples; but Yahweh's plans hold good for ever, the intentions of his heart from age to age."
                    Psalms 33[32]:10-11

In Situations of:

Impatience

"Our one desire is that every one of you should go on showing the same earnestness to the end, to the perfect fulfillment of our hopes, never growing careless, but imitating those who have the faith and the perseverance to inherit the promises."   **Hebrews 6:11-12**

"But that is not all we can boast about; we can boast about our sufferings. These sufferings bring patience, as we know, and patience brings perseverance, and perseverance brings hope, and this hope is not deeptive, because the love of God has been poured into our hearts by the Holy Spirit which has been given us."   **Romans 5:3-5**

"My brothers, you will always have your trials but, when they come, try to treat them as a happy privilege; you understand that your faith is only put to the test to make you patient, but patience too is to have its practical results so that you will become fully developed, complete, with nothing missing."   **James 1:2-4**

"Be as confident now, then, since the reward is so great. You will need endurance to do God's will and gain what he has promised. Only a little while now, a very little while, and the one that is coming will have come; he will not delay. The righteous man will live by faith."
                                        Hebrews 10:35-38a

"Now be patient, brothers, until the Lord's coming. Think of a farmer: how patiently he waits for the precious fruit of the ground until it has had the autumn rains and the spring rains! You too have to be patient; do not lose heart, because the Lord's coming will be soon."

James 5:7-8

"I waited and waited for Yahweh, now at last he has stooped to me and heard my cry for help. He has pulled me out of the horrible pit, out of the slough of the marsh, has settled my feet on a rock and steadied my steps."

Psalms 40[39]:1-2

"What the Spirit brings is very different: love, joy, peace, patience, kindness, goodness, trustfulness, gentlensess and self-control."

Galatians 5:22-23a

"It is good to wait in silence for Yahweh to save. [...] For the Lord does not reject mankind for ever and ever."

Lamentations 3:26.31

"Your endurance will win you your lives."

Luke 21:19

"He will repay each one as his works deserve. For those who sought renown and honor and immortality by always doing good there will be eternal life."

Romans 2:6-7

"That day, it will be said: See, this is our God in whom we hoped for salvation; Yahweh is the one in whom we hoped. We exult and we rejoice that he has saved us."

Isaiah 25:9

"Trust in Yahweh and do what is good, make your home in the land and live in peace; make Yahweh your only joy and he will give you what your heart desires. Commit your fate to Yahweh, trust in him and he will act."

Psalms 37[36]:3-5

"My son, if you aspire to serve the Lord, prepare yourself for an ordeal. Be sincere of heart, be steadfast, and do not be alarmed when disaster comes. Cling to him and do not leave him, so that you may be honored at the end of your days. Whatever happens to you, accept it, and in the uncertainties of your humble state, be patient, since gold is tested in the fire, and chosen men in the furnace of humiliation. Trust him and he will uphold you, follow a straight path and hope in him." **Ecclesiastcus 2:1-6**

"No, those who hope in you are never shamed."

Psalms 25[24]:3a

"What advantage has the wise man over the fool? And what about the pauper who keeps up appearances before his fellow men? Do appearances count more than the condition of the belly? This, too, is vanity and chasing of the wind." **Ecclesiastes 6:8-9**

In Situations of:

Dissatisfaction

"Do not worry about the wicked, do not envy those who do wrong. [...] Trust in Yahweh and do what is good, make your home in the land and live in peace; make Yahweh your only joy and he will give you what your heart desires."
Psalms 37[36]:1.3-4

"Thus says Yahweh who made you, who formed you from the womb, who is your help: Do not be afraid, Jacob my servant, Jeshurum whom I have chosen. For I will pour out water on the thirsty soil, streams on the dry ground. I will pour my spirit on your descendants, my blessing on your children." **Isaiah 44:2b-3**

"Bless Yahweh, my soul, bless his holy name, all that is in me! Bless Yahweh, my soul, and remember all his kindness: in forgiving all your offenses, in curing all your diseases, in redeeming your life from the Pit, in crowning you with love and tenderness, in filling your years with prosperity, in renewing your youth like an eagle's."
Psalms 103[102]:1-5

"I know how to be poor and I know how to be rich too. I have been through my initiation and now I am ready for anything anywhere: full stomach or empty stomach, powerty or plenty. There is nothing I cannot master with the help of the One who gives me strength." **Philippians 4:12-13**

"You will eat to your heart's content, will eat your fill, and praise the name of Yahweh your God who has treated you so wonderfully. (My people will not be disappointed any more)." **Joel 2:26**

"Yahweh, defend me for the sake of your name, rescue me, since your love is generous! Reduced to weakness and poverty, my heart is sorely tormented." **Psalms 109[108]:21-22**

"See now, he is the God of my salvation I have trust now and no fear, for Yahweh is my strength, my song, he is my salvation. And you will draw water joyfully from the springs of salvation." **Isaiah 12:2-3**

"Another man is a poor creature begging for assistance, badly off for support, but rich in poverty, and the Lord turns a favorable eye on him, sets him on his feet out of his abject condition, and enables him to hold his head high, to the utter amazement of many." **Ecclesiasticus 11:12-13**

"Happy those who hunger and thirst for what is right: they shall be satisfied." **Matthew 5:6**

"Do not be astonished at the sinner's achievements; trust the Lord and keep to your duty; since it is a trifle in the eyes of the Lord, in a moment, suddenly to make a poor man rich. The devout man receives the Lord's blessing as his reward, in a moment God brings his blessing to flower." **Ecclesiasticus 11:22-24**

Criticism

"The reason, therefore, why those who are in Christ Jesus are not condemned, is that the law of the spirit of life in Christ Jesus has set you free from the law of sin and death."
Romans 8:1-2

"And for anyone who is in Christ, there is a new creation; the old creation has gone, and now the new one is here."
II Corinthians 5:17

"For God sent his Son into the world not to condemn the world, but so that through him the world might be saved. No one who believes in him will be condemned; but whoever refuses to believe is condemned already, because he has refused to believe in the name of God's only Son."
John 3:17-18

"I tell you most solemnly, whoever listens to my words, and believes in the one who sent me, has eternal life; without being brought to judgment he has passed from death to life." **John 5:24**

"Let the wicked man abandon his way, the evil man his thoughts. Let him turn back to Yahweh who will take pity on him, to our God who is rich in forgiving."
Isaiah 55:7

"But if we acknowledge our sins, then God who is faithful and just will forgive our sins and purify us from everything that is wrong." **I John 1:9**

"Hard pressed, I invoked Yahweh, he heard me and came to my relief. With Yahweh on my side, I fear nothing: what can man do to me? With Yahweh on my side, best help of all, I can triumph over my enemies. I would rather take refuge in Yahweh than rely on men; I would rather take refuge in Yahweh than rely on princes."

Psalms 118[117]:5-9

"The salvation of the virtuous comes from Yahweh, he is their shelter when trouble comes; Yahweh helps and rescues them, he saves them because they take shelter in him."

Psalms 37[36]:39-40

"My dear people, you must not think it unaccountable that you should be tested by fire. There is nothing extraordinary in what has happened to you. If you can have some share in the sufferings of Christ, be glad, because you will enjoy a much greater gladness when his glory is revealed."

I Peter 4:12-13

"I was pressed, pressed, about to fall, but Yahweh came to my help; Yahweh is my strength and my song, he has been my savior."

Psalms 118[117]:13-14

"The good man wins the favor of Yahweh, but he condemns the man who is a schemer."

Proverbs 12:2

"Could anyone accuse those that God has chosen? When God aquits, could anyone condemn? Could Christ Jesus? No! He not only died for us – he rose from the dead, and there at God's right hand he stands and pleads for us."

Romans 8:33-34

"Then I heard a voice shout from heaven, 'Victory and power and empire for ever have been won by our God, and all authority for his Christ, now that the persecutor, who accused our brothers day and night before our God, has been brought down. They have triumphed over him by the blood of the Lamb and by the witness of their martyrdom, because even in the face of death they would not cling to life.'" **Revelation 12:10-11**

"'Neither do I condemn you,' said Jesus, 'go away and don't sin any more.'" **John 8:11b**

"There will be no further need for neighbor to try to teach neighbor, or brother to say to brother, 'Learn to know Yahweh!' No, they will all know me, the least no less than the greatest [...] since I will forgive their iniquity and never call their sin to mind." **Jeremiah 31:34**

"If you come back sincerely to Yahweh, your brothers and your sons will win favor with their conquerors and return to this land, for Yahweh your God is gracious and merciful. If you come back to him, he will not turn his face from you." **II Chronicles 30:9**

"The spirit of the Lord Yahweh has been given to me, for Yahweh has anointed me. He has sent me to bring good news to the poor, to bind up hearts that are broken; to proclaim liberty to captives, freedom to those in prison." **Isaiah 61:1**

"While Yahweh himself ransoms the souls of his servants, and those who take shelter in him have nothing to pay." **Psalms 34[33]:22**

"The wicked man spies on the virtuous, seeking to kill him; Yahweh will never leave him in those clutches, or let him be condemned under trial." **Psalms 37[36]:32-33**

"Not a weapon forged against you will succed. Every tongue that accuses you in judgment will be refuted. Such will be the lot of the servants of Yahweh, the triumphs I award them – it is Yahweh who speaks." **Isaiah 54:17**

"Then you can invoke me in your troubles and I will rescue you, and you shall honor me."
Psalms 50[49]:15

In Situations of:

Confusion

"God is not a God of disorder but of peace."
I Corinthians 14:33

"I waited and waited for Yahweh, now at last he has stooped to me and heard my cry for help. He has pulled me out of the horrible pit, out of the slough of the marsh, has settled my feet on a rock and steadied my steps. He has put a new song in my mouth, a song of praise to our God."
Psalms 40[39]:1-3a

"Look at the generations of old and see: who ever trusted in the Lord and was put to shame? Or who ever feared him steadfastly and was left forsaken? Or who ever called out to him, and was ignored?" **Ecclesiasticus 2:11-12**

"Our help is in the name of Yahweh, who made heaven and earth." **Psalms 124[123]:8**

"Wherever you find jealousy and ambition, you find disharmony, and wicked things of every kind being done; whereas the wisdom that comes down from above is essentially something pure; it also makes for peace, and is kindly and considerate; it is full of compassion and shows itself by doing good; nor is there any trace of partiality or hypocrisy in it. Peacemakers, when they work for peace, sow the seeds which will bear fruit in holiness."
James 3:16-18

"If there is any one of you who needs wisdom, he must ask God, who gives to all freely and ungrudgingly; it will be given to him." **James 1:5**

"Trust wholeheartedly in Yahweh, put no faith in your own perception; in every course you take, have him in mind: he will see that your paths are smooth." **Proverbs 3:5-6**

"You will have to suffer only for a little while: the God of all grace who called you to eternal glory in Christ will see that all is well again: he will confirm, strengthen and supporyou." **I Peter 5:10**

"You, Israel, my servant [...]; you to whom I said, 'you are my servant. I have chosen you, not rejected you,' do not be afraid, for I am with you; stop being anxious and watchful, for I am your God. I give you strength, I bring you help, I uphold you with my victorious right hand." **Isaiah 41:8a.9b-10**

"When scripture says: those who believe in him with have no cause for shame, it makes no distinction between Jew and Greek: all belong to the same Lord who is rich enough, however many ask his help, for everyone who calls on the name of the Lord will be saved." **Romans 10:11-13**

"Unload your burden on to Yahweh, and he will support you; he will never permit the virtuous to falter." **Psalms 55[54]:22**

"Should you pass through the sea, I will be with you; or through rivers, they will not swallow you up. Should you walk through fire, you will not be scorched and the flames will not burn you. For I am Yahweh, your God, the Holy One of Israel, your savior." **Isaiah 43:2-3a**

"Whether you turn to right or left, your ears will hear these words behind you, 'This is the way, follow it.'"
Isaiah 30:21

"Do not be afraid of them therefore. For everything that is now covered will be uncovered, and everything now hidden will be made clear." **Matthew 10:26**

In Situations of:
Trial and Tribulation

"Do not let your hearts be troubled. Trust in God still, and trust in me. [...] Peace I bequeath to you, my own peace I give you, a peace the world cannot give, this is my gift to you. Do not let your hearts be troubled or afraid."
John 14:1.27

"Universal peace for those who love your Law, no stumbling blocks for them!" **Psalms 119[118]:165**

"Every face turned to him grows brighter and is never ashamed. A cry goes up from the poor man, and Yahweh hears, and helps him in all his troubles."
Psalms 34[33]:5-6

"God is our shelter, our strength, ever ready to help in time of trouble, so we shall not be afraid when the earth gives way, when mountains tumble into the depths of the sea, and its waters roar and seethe, the mountains tottering as it heaves. (Yahweh Sabaoth is on our side, our citadel, the God of Jacob!)" **Psalms 46[45]:1-3**

"We are in difficulties on all sides, but never cornered; we see no answer to our problems, but never despair; we have been persecuted, but never deserted; knocked down, but never killed [...]. Knowing that he who raised the Lord Jesus to life will raise us with Jesus in our turn, and put us by his side and you with us. [...] That is why there is no weakening on our part, and instead, though this outer man of ours may be falling into decay, the inner man is renewed day by day." **II Corinthians 4:8-9.14.16**

155

"Happy indeed the man whom God corrects! Then do not refuse this lesson from Shaddai. For he who wounds is he who soothes the sore, and the hand that hurts is the hand that heals. Six times he will deliver you from sorrow, and the seventh, evil shall not touch you."

Job 5:17-19

"Then they called to Yahweh in their trouble and he rescued them from their sufferings."

Psalms 107[106]:19

"Yahweh is good; he is a stronghold in the day of distress; he calls to mind those who trust in him."

Nahum 1:7

"We know that by turning everything to their good God co-operates with all those who love him, with all those that he has called according to his purpose."

Romans 8:28

"There is no need to worry; but if there is anything you need, pray for it, asking God for it with prayer and thanksgiving, and that peace of God, which is so much greater than we can understand, will guard your hearts and your thoughts, in Christ Jesus." **Philippians 4:6-7**

"Yes, the troubles which are soon over, though they weigh little, train us for the carrying of a weight of eternal glory which is out of all proportion to them. And so we have no eyes for things that are visible, but only for things that are invisible; for visible things last only for a time, and the invisible things are eternal." **II Corinthians 4:17-18**

In Situations of:

Illness

"If one of you is ill, he should send for the elders of the church, and they must anoint him with oil in the name of the Lord and pray over him. The prayer of faith will save the sick man and the Lord will raise him up again; and if he has committed any sins, he will be forgiven."
James 5:14-15

"If you listen carefully to the voice of Yahweh your God and do what is right in his eyes, if you pay attention to his commandments and keep his statutes, I shall inflict on you none of the evils that I inflicted on the Egyptians, for it is I, Yahweh, who give you healing."   **Exodus 15:26**

"Hope of Israel, Yahweh! All who abandon you will be put to shame, those who turn from you will be uprooted from the land, since they have abandoned the fountain of living water. Heal me, Yahweh, and I shall be really healed, save me, and I shall be saved, for you alone are my hope."
Jeremiah 17:13-14

"And everyone in the crowd was trying to touch him because power came out of him that cured them all."
Luke 6:19

"Why bother to complain about your wound? Your pain is incurable. So great is your guilt, so many your sins, that I have done all this to you. [...] But I will restore you to health and heal your wounds – it is Yahweh who speaks."
Jeremiah 30:15.17a

"No herb, no poultice cured them, but it was your word, Lord, which heals all things."   **Wisdom 16:12**

"How differently with your people! You gave them the food of angels, from heaven untiringly sending them bread already prepared, containing every delight, satisfying every taste. [...] So that your beloved children, Lord, might learn that the various crops are not what nourishes man, but your word which preserves all who trust in you."
Wisdom 16:20.26

"Come, let us return to Yahweh. He has torn us to pieces, but he will heal us; he has struck us down, but he will bandage our wounds."   **Hosea 6:1-2**

"My son, pay attention to my words, listen carefully to the words I say; do not let them out of your sight, keep them deep in your heart. They are life to those who grasp them, health for the entire body."   **Proverbs 4:20-22**

"My son, when you are ill, do not be depressed, but pray to the Lord and he will heal you. Renounce your faults, keep your hands unsoiled, and cleanse your heart from all sin."   **Ecclesiasticus 38:9-10**

"He was bearing our faults in his own body on the cross, so that we might die to our faults and live for holiness; through his wounds you have been healed."
I Peter 2:24

"Bless Yahweh, my soul, and remember all his kindnesses: in forgiving all your offenses, in curing all your diseases, in redeeming your life from the Pit, in crowning you with love and tenderness."   **Psalms 103[102]:2-4**

"And yet ours were the sufferings he bore, ours the sorrows he carried. But we, we thought of him as someone punished, struck by God, and brought low. Yet he was pierced through for our faults, crushed for our sins. On him lies a punishment that brings us peace, and through his wounds we are healed." **Isaiah 53:4-5**

"Then they called to Yahweh in their trouble and he rescued them from their sufferings; sending his word and curing them, he snatchead them from the Pit."
Psalms 107[106]:19-20

"I tell you therefore: everything you ask and pray for, believe that you have it already, and it will be yours. And when you stand in prayer, forgive whatever you have against anybody, so that your Father in heaven may forgive your failings too." **Marcos 11:24-25**

"'If you can?' retorted Jesus. 'Everything is possible for anyone who has faith.' Immediately the father of the boy cried out, 'I do have faith. Help the little faith I have!'"
Mark 9:23-24

"These are the signs that will be associated with believers: in my name they will cast out devils; they will have the gift of tongues; thet will pick up snakes in their hands, and be unharmed should they drink deadly poison; they will lay their hands on the sick, who will recover."
Mark 16:17-18

In Situations of:

Fear

"Peace I bequeath to you, my own peace I give you, a peace the world cannot give, this is my gift to you. Do not let your hearts be troubled or afraid."   **John 14:27**

"In peace I lie down, and fall asleep at once, since you alone, Yahweh, make me rest secure." **Psalms 4:8**

"God's gift was not a spirit of timidity, but the Spirit of power and love and self-control."   **II Timothy 1:7**

"In love there can be no fear, but fear is driven out by perfect love: because to fear is to expect punishment, and anyone who is afraid is still imperfect in love."
I John 4:18

"Yahweh is my shepherd, I lack nothing. [...] Though I pass through a gloomy valley, I fear no harm; beside me your rod and your staff are there, to hearten me."
Psalms 23[22]:1.4

"The spirit you received is not the spirit of slaves bringing fear into your lives again; it is the spirit of sons, and it makes us cry out, 'Abba, Father!'"
Romans 8:15

"And so we can say with confidence: With the Lord to help me, I fear nothing: what can man do to me?"
Hebrews 13:6

"If you live in the shelter of Elyon and make your home in the shadow of Shaddai, you can say to Yahweh, 'My refuge, my fortress, my God in whom I trust!' He rescues you from the snares of fowlers hoping to destroy you; he covers you with his feathers, and you find shelter underneath his wings."
Psalms 91[90]:1-4

"You need not fear the terrors of night, the arrow that flies in the daytime, the plague that stalks in the dark, the scourge that wreaks havoc in broad daylight. [...] You who can say, 'Yahweh my refuge,' and make Elyon your fortress. No disaster can overtake you, no plague come near your tent: he will put you in his angels' charge to guard you wherever you go."
Psalms 91[90]:5-6.9-11

"Do not be afraid, for I am with you; stop being anxious and watchful, for I am your God. I give you strength, I bring you help, I uphold you with my victorious right hand."
Isaiah 41:10

"When you sit down, you will not be afraid, when you lie down, sweet will be your sleep. Have no fear of sudden terror or of assault from wicked men, since Yahweh will be your guarantor, he will keep your steps from the snare."
Proverbs 3:24-26

"Have no fear! Stand firm, and you will see what Yahweh will do to save you today: the Egyptians you see today, you will never see again. Yahweh will do the fighting for you: you have only to keep still."
Exodus 14:13b-14

"When I am most afraid, I put my trust in you; in God, whose word I praise, in God I put my trust, fearing nothing;

161

what can men do to me? Then my enemies will have to fall back as soon as I call for help. This I know: that God is on my side." **Psalms 56[55]:3-4.9**

"Be strong, stand firm, have no fear of them, no terror, for Yahweh your God is going with you; he will not fail you or desert you." **Deuteronomy 31:6**

"Should you pass through the sea, I will be with you; or through rivers, they will not swallow you up. Should you walk through fire, you will not be scorched and the flames will not burn you. For I am Yahweh, your God, the Holy One of Israel, your savior." **Isaiah 43:2-3a**

"To be afraid of men is a snare, he who puts his trust in Yahweh is secure." **Proverbs 29:25**

"Yahweh is my light and my salvation, whom need I fear? Yahweh is the fortress of my life, of whom should I be afraid?" **Psalms 27[26]:1**

"Not a weapon forged against you will succeed. Every tongue that accuses you in judgment will be refuted. Such will be the lot of the servants of Yahweh, the triumphs I award them – it is Yahweh who speaks." **Isaiah 54:17**

"He called those he intended for this; those he called he justified, and with those he justified he shared his glory. After saying this, what can we add? With God on our side who can be against us?" **Romans 8:30-31**

"In my alarm I exclaimed, 'I have been matched out of your sight!' Yet you heard my petition when I called to you for help. Love Yahweh, all you devout: Yahweh, protector of the faithful." **Psalms 31[30]:22-23a**

"Yahweh guards you, shades you. With Yahweh at your right hand sun cannot strike you down by day, nor moon at night. Yahweh guards you from harm, he guards your lives, he guards you leaving, coming back, now and for always." **Psalms 121[120]:5-8**

"The man who fears the Lord will not be fainthearted, will not be daunted since the Lord is his hope." **Ecclesiasticus 34:16**

"Jesus called out to them, saying, 'Courage! It is I! Do not be afraid.'" **Matthew 14:27**

In Situations of:

Rebellion

"To the rest of you I say: do what the elders tell you, and all wrap yourselves in humility to be servants of each other, because God refuses the proud and will always favor the humble. Bow down, then, before the power of God now, and he will raise you up on the appointed day."

I Peter 5:5-6

"But if at heart you have the bitterness of jealousy, or a self-seeking ambition, never make any claims for yourself or cover up the truth with lies – principles of this kind are not the wisdom that comes down from above: they are only earthly, animal and devilish. Wherever you find jealousy and ambition, you find disharmony, and wicked things of every kind being done [...]. Peacemakers, when they work for peace, sow the seeds which will bear fruit in holiness."

James 3:14-16.18

"Free your minds, then, of encumbrances; control them, and put your trust in nothing but the grace that will be given you when Jesus Christ is revealed. Do not behave in the way that you liked to before you learned the truth; make a habit of obedience." **I Peter 1:13-14**

"'If you are willing to obey, you shall eat the good things of the earth. But if you persist in rebellion, the sword shall eat you instead.' The mouth of Yahweh has spoken."

Isaiah 1:19-20

"Obey your leaders and do as they tell you, because they must give an account of the way they look after your souls; make this a joy for them to do, and not a grief – you yourselves would be the losers." **Hebrews 13:17**

"Is the pleasure of Yahweh in holocausts and sacrifices or in obedience to the voice of Yahweh? Yes, obedience is better than sacrifice, submissiveness better than the fat of rams. Rebellion is a sin of sorcery. Presumption a crime of teraphim." **I Samuel 15:22b-23a**

"For the sake of the Lord, accept the authority of every social institution: the emperor, as the supreme authority, and the governors as commissioned by him to punish criminals and praise good citizenship. God wants you to be good citizens, so as to silence what fools are saying in their ignorance." **I Peter 2:13-15**

"In particular, I want to urge you in the name of the Lord, not to go on living the aimless kind of life that pagans live. Intellectually they are in the dark, and they are estranged from the life of God, without knowledge because they have shut their hearts to it." **Ephesians 4:17-18**

"You were darkness once, but now you are light in the Lord; be like children of light, for the effects of the light are seen in complete goodness and right living and truth. Try to discover what the Lord wants of you, having nothing to do with the futile works of darkness but exposing them by contrast." **Ephesians 5:8-11**

"So be very careful about the sort of lives you lead, like intelligent and not like senseless people. This may be a wicked age, but your lives should redeem it. And do not be thoughtless but recognize what is the will of the Lord. Do not drug yourselves with wine; this is simply dissipation; be filled with the Spirit." **Ephesians 5:15-18**

"Our war is not fought with weapons of flesh, yet they are strong enough, in God's cause, to demolish fortresses. We demolish sophistries, and the arrogance that tries to resist the knowledge of God; every thought is our prisoner, captured to be brought into obedience to Christ."
II Corinthians 10:4-5

"Very soon now, I shall be with you again, bringing the reward to be given to every man according to what he deserves. I am the Alpha and the Omega, the First and the Last, the Beginning and the End. Happy are those who will have washed their robes clean, so that they will have the right to feed on the tree of life and can come through the gates into the city." **Revelation 22:12-14**

"Come back, disloyal children [...], for I alone am your Master. I will take one from a town, two from a clan, and bring you to Zion. I will give you shepherds after my own heart, and these shall feed you on knowledge and discretion."
Jeremiah 3:14-15

"A noise is heard on the bare heights: the weeping and entreaty of the sons of Israel, because they have gone so wildly astray, and forgotten Yahweh their God. 'Come back, disloyal sons, I want to heal your disloyalty.' 'We are here, we are coming to you, for you are Yahweh our God.'"
Jeremiah 3:21-22

"Give in to God, then; resist the devil, and he will run away from you." **James 4:7**

In Situations of:

Revolt

"Remember this, my dear brothers: be quick to listen but slow to speak and slow to rouse your temper; God's righteousness is never served by man's anger."

James 1:19-20

"Even if you are angry, you must not sin: never let the sun set on your anger or else you will give the devil a foothold. [...] Guard against foul talk; let your words be for the improvement of others, as occasion offers, and do good to your listeners, otherwise you will only be grieving the Holy Spirit of God who has marked you with his seal for you to be set free when the day comes."   **Ephesians 4:26-27.29-30**

"A mild answer turns away wrath, sharp words stir up anger. [...] The ear attentive to wholesome correction finds itself at home in the company of the wise. [...] The fear of Yahweh is a school of wisdom, humility goes before honor."

Proverbs 15:1.31.33

"Yes, if you forgive others their failings, your heavenly Father will forgive you yours."   **Matthew 6:14**

"The equable man is full of discernment, the hasty is more than foolish. The life of the body is a tranquil heart."

Proverbs 14:29-30a

"Kindly words are a honeycomb, sweet to the taste, wholesome to the body. [...] Better an equable man than a hero, a man master of himself than one who takes a city."
Proverbs 16:24.32

"Better the end of a matter than its beginning, better patience than pride. Do not be hasty with your resentment, for resentment is found in the heart of fools."
Ecclesiastes 7:8-9

"Never try to get revenge; leave that, my friends, to God's anger. As scripture says: Vengeance is mine – I will pay them back, the Lord promises." **Romans 12:19**

"If your enemy is hungry, give him something to eat; if thirsty, something to drink. By this you heap red-hot coals on his head, and Yahweh will reward you."
Proverbs 25:21-22

"We are all aware who it was that said: Vengeance is mine; I will repay. And again: The Lord will judge his people." **Hebrews 10:30**

"Never have grudges against others, or lose your temper, or raise your voice to anybody, or call each other names, or allow any sort of spitefulness. Be friends with one another, and kind, forgiving each other as readily as God forgave you in Christ." **Ephesians 4:31-32**

"But I say this to you: anyone who is angry with his brother will answer for it before the court; if a man calls his brother 'Fool' he will answer for it before the Sanhedrin;

168

and if a man calls him 'Renegade' he will answer for it in hell fire. So then, if you are bringing your offering to the altar and there remember that your brother has something against you, leave your offering there before the altar, go and be reconciled with your brother first, and then come back and present your offering." **Matthew 5:22-24**

"And when you stand in prayer, forgive whatever you have against anybody, so that your Father in heaven may forgive your failings too. [But if you do not forgive, your Father in heaven will not forgive your failings either.]"
Mark 11:25-26

"He who exacts vengeance will experience the vengeance of the Lord, who keeps strict account of sin. Forgive your neighbor the hurt he does you, and when you pray, your sins will be forgiven. If a man nurses anger against another, can he then demand compassion from the Lord? Showing no pity for a man like himself, can he then plead for his own sins? Mere creature of flesh, he cherishes resentment; who will forgive him his sins?"
Ecclesiasticus 28:1-5

"But now you, of all people, must give all these things up: getting angry, being bad-tempered, spitefulness, abusive language and dirty talk; and never tell each other lies. You have stripped off your old behavior with your old self, and you have put on a new self which will progress toward true knowledge the more it is renewed in the image of its creator."
Colossians 3:8-10

"Because there will be judgment without mercy for those who have not been merciful themselve; but the merciful need have no fear of judgment." **James 2:13**

"Enough of anger, leave rage aside, do not worry, nothing but evil can come of it: for the wicked will be expelled, while those who hope in Yahweh shall have the land for their own. A little longer, and the wicked will be no more, search his place well, he will not be there; but the humble shall have the land for their own to enjoy untroubled peace."   **Psalms 37[36]:8-11**

In Situations of:

Sadness and Desolation

"Blessed be the God and Father of our Lord Jesus Christ, a gentle Father and the God of all consolation, who comforts us in all our sorrows, so that we can offer others, in their sorrows, the consolation that we have received from God ourselves."   **II Corinthians 1:3-4**

"Shout for joy, you heavens; exult, you earth! You mountains, break into happy cries! For Yahweh consoles his people and takes pity on those who are afflicted."
Isaiah 49:13

"We want you to be quite certain, brothers, about those who have died, to make sure that you do not grieve about them, like the other people who have no hope. We believe that Jesus died and rose again, and that it will be the same for those who have died in Jesus: God will bring them with him."   **I Thessalonians 4:13-14**

"For we know that when the tent that we live in on earth is folded up, there is a house built by God for us, an everlasting home not made by human hands, in the heavens. [...] This is the purpose for which God made us, and he has given us the pledge of the Spirit."   **II Corinthians 5:1.5**

"But the souls of the virtuous are in the hands of God, no torment shall ever touch them. In the eyes of the unwise, they did appear to die, their going looked like a disaster, their leaving us, like annihilation; but they are in peace."
Wisdom 3:1-3

171

"But the virtuous live for ever, their recompense lies with the Lord. The Most High takes care of them."

Wisdom 5:15

"Is God-with-them. He will wipe away all tears from their eyes; there will be no more death, and no more mourning or sadness. The world of the past has gone."

Revelation 21:3c-4

"Those who acknowledge your name can rely on you, you never desert those who seek you, Yahweh."

Psalms 9:10

"This has been my comfort in my suffering: that your promise gives me life."   **Psalms 119[118]:50**

"I, I am your consoler. How then can you be afraid of mortal man, of son of man, whose fate is the fate of grass?"

Isaiah 51:12

"I think that what we suffer in this life can never be compared to the glory, as yet unrevealed, which is waiting for us."   **Romans 8:18**

"May our Lord Jesus Christ himself, and God our Father who has given us his love and, through his grace, such inexhaustible comfort and such sure hope."

II Thessalonians 2:16

"No longer are you to be named 'Forsaken,' nor your land 'Abandoned,' but you shall be called 'My Delight,' and your land 'The Wedded'; for Yahweh takes delight in you and your land will have its wedding."

Isaiah 62:4

"Death is swallowed up in victory. Death, where is your victory? Death, where is your sting? Now the sting of death is sin, and sin gets its power from the Law. So let us thank God for giving us the victory through our Lord Jesus Christ."

I Corinthians 15:54d-57

"We teach what scripture calls: the things that no eye has seen and no ear has heard, things beyond the mind of man, all that God has prepared for those who love him."

I Corinthians 2:9

"Arise, shine out, for your light has come, the glory of Yahweh is rising on you. [...] No more will the sun give you daylight, nor moonlight shine on you, but Yahweh will be your everlasting light, your God will be your splendor. Your sun will set no more nor your moon wane, but Yahweh will be your everlasting light and your days of mourning will be ended."

Isaiah 60:1.19-20

"That day, you will say: I give thanks to you, Yahweh, you were angry with me but your anger is appeased and you have given me consolation. See now, he is the God of my salvation I have trust now and no fear, for Yahweh is my strength, my song, he is my salvation."

Isaiah 12:1-2

"Death came through one man and in the same way the resurrection of the dead has come through one man. Just as all men die in Adam, so all men will be brought to life in Christ."

I Corinthians 15:21-22

"Jesus said: 'I am the resurrection. If anyone believes in me, even though he dies he will live, and whoever lives and believes in me will never die. Do you believe this?'"

John 11:25-26

"Then, seeing this, the humble can rejoice: long life to your hearts, all you who seek for God! Yahweh will always hear those who are in need, will never scorn his captive people." **Psalms 69[68]:32-33**

"Happy the gentle: they shall have the earth for their heritage." **Matthew 5:4**

When Guidance:

Is Necessary

"Whether you turn to right or left, your ears will hear these words behind you, 'This is the way, follow it.'"
Isaiah 30:21

"But when the Spirit of truth comes he will lead you to the complete truth, since he will not be speaking as from himself but will say only what he has learned; and he will tell you of the things to come." **John 16:13**

"Yahweh guides a man's steps, they are sure, and he takes pleasure in his progress." **Psalms 37[36]:23**

"Let me put it like this: if you are guided by the Spirit you will be in no danger of yielding to self-indulgence. [...] Since the Spirit is our life, let us be directed by the Spirit."
Galatians 5:16.25

"It shall be said: Open up, open up, clear the way, remove all obstacles from the way of my people. [...]; but I have seen the way he went. 'But I will heal him, and console him. I will comfort him to the full, both him and his afflicted fellows, bringing praise to their lips.'"
Isaiah 57:14.18-19a

"God, in your temple we reflect on your love [...]. That God is here, our God and leader, for ever and ever."
Psalms 48[47]:9.14

"Yahweh is so good, so upright, he teaches the way to sinners; in all that is right he guides the humble, and instructs the poor in his way." **Psalms 25[24]:8-9**

"Even so, I stayed in your presence, you held my right hand; now guide me with advice and in the end receive me into glory." **Psalms 73[72]:23-24**

"In every course you take, have him in mind: he will see that your paths are smooth." **Proverbs 3:6**

"Everyone who fears Yahweh will be taught the course a man should choose." **Psalms 25[24]:12**

"But I will make the blind walk along the road and lead them along paths. I will turn darkness into light before them and rocky places into level tracks. 'These things I will do, and not leave them undone.'" **Isaiah 42:16**

"A man's conduct may strike him as pure, Yahweh, however, weighs the motives. Commend what you do to Yahweh, and your plans will find achievement." **Proverbs 16:2-3**

"A man's heart plans out his way but it is Yahweh who makes his steps secure. [...] To turn from evil is the way of honest men; he keeps his life safe who watches where he goes." **Proverbs 16:9.17**

"Then they called to Yahweh in their trouble and he rescued them from their sufferings, guiding them by a route leading direct to an inhabited town." **Psalms 107[106]:6-7**

"Thus says Yahweh, your redeemer, the Holy One of Israel: I, Yahweh, your God, teach you what is good for you, I lead you in the way that you must go."

Isaiah 48:17

"Yahweh will always guide you, giving you relief in desert places. He will give strength to your bones and you shall be like a watered garden, like a spring of water whose waters never run dry."

Isaiah 58:11

2

The Word of God for the Family

Marriage

"Yahweh God said, 'It is not good that the man should be alone. I will make him a helpmate.'"

Genesis 2:18

"But from the beginning of creation God made them male and female. This is why a man must leave father and mother, and the two become one body. They are no longer two, therefore, but one body. So then, what God has united, man must not divide."   **Mark 10:7-9**

"For this reason, a man must leave his father and mother and be joined to his wife, and the two will become one body. This mystery has many implications; but I am saying it applies to Christ and the Church. To sum up; you too, each one of you, must love his wife as he loves himself; and let every wife respect her husband."

Ephesians 5:31-33

"Thus, if you fear Yahweh your God all the days of your life and if you keep all his laws and commandments which I lay on you, you will have a long life, you and your son and your grandson." **Deuteronomy 6:2**

"Have you not read that the creator from the beginning made them male and female and that he said: This is why a man must leave father and mother, and cling to his wife, and the two become one body? They are no longer two, therefore, but one body. So then, what God has united, man must not divide." **Matthew 19:4b-6**

"Marriage is to be honored by all, and marriages are to be kept undefiled, because fornicators and adulterers will come under God's judgment." **Hebrews 13:4**

"Take wives and have sons and daughters; choose wives for your sons, find husbands for your daughters so that these can bear sons and daughters in their turn; you must increase there and not decrease." **Jeremiah 29:6**

"Now for the questions about which you wrote. Yes, it is a good thing for a man not to touch a woman; but since sex is always a danger, let each man have his own wife and each woman her own husband. The husband must give his wife what she has the right to expect, and so too the wife to the

180

husband. The wife has no rights over her own body; it is the husband who has them. In the same way, the husband has no rights over his body; the wife has them. Do not refuse each other except by mutual consent, and then only for an agreed time, to leave yourselves free for prayer; then come together again in case Satan should take advantage of your weakness to tempt you." **I Corinthians 7:1-5**

"And each one of you to know how to use the body that belongs to him in a way that is holy and honorable, not giving way to selfish lust like the pagans who do not know God. He wants nobody at all ever to sin by taking advantage of a brother in these matters; the Lord always punishes sin of that sort, as we told you before and assured you." **I Thessalonians 4:4-6**

"I think it is best for young widows to marry again and have children and a home to look after, and not give the enemy any chance to raise a scandal about them." **I Timothy 5:14**

"In the same way, wives should be obedient to their husbands. Then, if there are some husbands who have not yet obeyed the word, they may find themselves won over, without a word spoken, by the way their wives behave, when they see how faithful and conscientious they are. [...]

In the same way, husbands must always treat their wives with consideration in their life together, respecting a woman as one who, though she may be the weaker partner, is equally an heir to the life of grace. This will stop anything from coming in the way of your prayers." **I Peter 3:1-2.7**

"For the married I have something to say, and this is not from me but from the Lord: a wife must not leave her husband – or if she does leave him, she must either remain unmarried or else make it up with her husband – nor must a husband send his wife away. The rest is from me and not from the Lord. If a brother has a wife who is an unbeliever, and she is content to live with him, he must not send her away."   **I Corinthians 7:10-12**

"Who finds a wife finds happiness, receiving a mark of favor from Yahweh."   **Proverbs 18:22**

"They told him, 'Become a believer in the Lord Jesus, and you will be saved, and your household too.'"
                        Acts 16:31

Wives

"A perfect wife – who can find her? She is far beyond the price of pearls. Her husband's heart has confidence in her, from her he will derive no little profit. Advantage and not hurt she brings him all the days of her life.

[...] She is clothed in strength and dignity, she can laugh at the days to come. When she opens her mouth, she does so wisely; on her tongue is kindly instruction. She keeps good watch on the conduct of her household, no bread of idleness for her. Her sons stand up and proclaim her blessed, her husband, too, sings her praises: 'Many women have done admirable things, but you surpass them all!' Charm is deceitful, and beauty empty; the woman who is wise is the one to praise."   **Proverbs 31:10-12.25-30**

"The grace of a wife will charm her husband, her accomplishments will make him the stronger. A silent wife is a gift from the Lord, no price can be put on a well-trained character. A modest wife is a boon twice over, a chaste character cannot be weighed on scales. Like the sun rising over the mountains of the Lord is the beauty of a good wife in a well-kept house."   **Ecclesiasticus 26:16-21**

"Who finds a wife finds happiness, receiving a mark of favor from Yahweh."   **Proverbs 18:22**

"Spend your life with the woman you love, through all the fleeting days of the life that God has given you under the sun; for this is the lot assigned to you in life and in the efforts you exert under the sun."   **Ecclesiastes 9:9**

"Happy the husband of a really good wife; the number of his days will be doubled. A perfect wife is the joy of her husband, he will live out the years of his life in peace. A good wife is the best of portions, reserved for those who fear the Lord; rich or poor, they will be glad of heart, cheerful of face, whatever the season."   **Ecclesiasticus 26:1-4**

"From fathers comes inheritance of house and wealth, from Yahweh a wife who is discreet."

Proverbs 19:14

"A good wife, her husband's crown, a shameless wife, a cancer in his bones."   **Proverbs 12:4**

"Wives should regard their husbands as they regard the Lord, since as Christ is head of the Church and saves the whole body, so is a husband the head of his wife; and as the Church submits to Christ, so should wives to their husbands, in everything."   **Ephesians 5:22-24**

"Wives, give way to your husbands, as you should in the Lord."   **Colossians 3:18**

"In the same way, wives should be obedient to their husbands. Then, if there are some husbands who have not yet obeyed the word, they may find themselves won over, without a word spoken, by the way their wives behave, when they see how faithful and conscientious they are. Do not dress up for show: doing up your hair, wearing gold bracelets and fine clothes; all this should be inside, in a person's heart, imperishable: the ornament of a sweet and gentle disposition – this is what is precious in the sight of God."

I Peter 3:1-4

Husbands

"Let these words of mine remain in your heart and in your soul; fasten them on your hand as a sign and on your forehead as a circlet. Teach them to your children and say them over to them, whether at rest in your house or walking abroad, at your lying down or at your rising. Write them on the doorposts of your house and on your gates, so that you and your children may live long in the land that Yahweh swore to your fathers he would give them for as long as there is a sky above the earth." **Deuteronomy 11:18-21**

"Husbands should love their wives just as Christ loved the Church and sacrificed himself for her to make her holy. He made her clean by washing her in water with a form of words, so that when he took her to himself she would be glorious, with no speck or wrinkle or anything like that, but holy and faultless.

In the same way, husbands must love their wives as they love their own bodies; for a man to love his wife is for him to love himself. A man never hates his own body, but he feeds it and looks after it; and that is the way Christ treats the Church, because it is his body – and we are its living parts. For this reason, a man must leave his father and mother and be joined to his wife, and the two will become one body.

This mystery has many implications; but I am saying it applies to Christ and the Church. To sum up; you too, each one of you, must love his wife as he loves himself; and let every wife respect her husband." **Ephesians 5:25-33**

"For I have singled him out to command his sons and his household after him to maintain the way of Yahweh by just and upright living. In this way Yahweh will carry out for Abraham what he has promised him." **Genesis 18:19**

"Yahweh stands as witness between you and the wife of your youth, the wife with whom you have broken faith, even though she was your partner and your wife by covenant. Did he not create a single being that has flesh and the breath of life? And what is this single being destined for? God-given offspring. Be careful for your own life, therefore, and do not break faith with the wife of your youth."

Malachi 2:14b-15

"Husbands, love your wives and treat them with gentleness. Children, be obedient to your parents always, because that is what will please the Lord."

Colossians 3:19-20

"The husband must give his wife what she has the right to expect, and so too the wife to the husband."

I Corinthians 7:3

"Let these words I urge on you today be written on your heart. You shall repeat them to your children and say them over to them whether at rest in your house or walking abroad, at your lying down or at your rising; you shall fasten them on your hand as a sign and on your forehead as a circlet; you shall write them on the doorposts of your house and on your gates." **Deuteronomy 6:6-9**

"The father of the virtuous man will rejoice indeed, he who fathers a wise man will have joy of it."

Proverbs 23:24

186

"The crown of the aged is their children's children; the children's glory is their father."

Proverbs 17:6

"A wise son is his father's joy, a foolish man despises his mother." **Proverbs 15:20**

"Parents, never drive your children to resentment or you will make them feel frustrated."

Colossians 3:21

"The good man bequeaths his heritage to his children's children, the wealth of the sinner is stored up for the virtuous." **Proverbs 13:22**

"The man who fails to use the stick hates his son; the man who is free with his correction loves him."

Proverbs 13:24

"In the same way, husbands must always treat their wives with consideration in their life together, respecting a woman as one who, though she may be the weaker partner, is equally an heir to the life of grace. This will stop anything from coming in the way of your prayers."

I Peter 3:7

"Happy, all those who fear Yahweh and follow in his paths. You will eat what your hands have worked for, happiness and prosperity will be yours. Your wife: a fruitful vine on the inner walls of your house. Your sons: around your table like shoots around an olive tree.

Such are the blessings that fall on the man who fears Yahweh. May Yahweh bless you from Zion, all the days of your life! May you see Jerusalem prosperous and live to see your children's children! Peace to Israel!"

Psalms 128[127]

"Spend your life with the woman you love, through all the fleeting days of the life that God has given you under the sun; for this is the lot assigned to you in life and in the efforts you exert under the sun."   **Ecclesiastes 9:9**

"And may your fountainhead be blessed! Find joy with the wife you married in your youth, fair as a hind, graceful as a fawn. Let hers be the company you keep, hers the breasts that ever fill you with delight, hers the love that ever holds you captive."   **Proverbs 5:18-19**

"Anyone who does not look after his own relations, especially if they are living with him, has rejected the faith and is worse than an unbeliever."   **I Timothy 5:8**

"However, what I want you to understand is that Christ is the head of every man, man is the head of woman, and God is the head of Christ."   **I Corinthians 11:3**

Children

"Keep your father's principle, my son, do not spurn your mother's teaching. Bind them ever to your heart, tie them around your neck. When you walk, these will guide you, when you lie down, watch over you, when you wake, talk with you."
Proverbs 6:20-22

"He who honors his mother is like someone amassing a fortune. Whoever respects his father will be happy with children of his own, he shall be heard on the day when he prays."
Ecclesiasticus 3:5-6

"Listen, my son, to your father's instruction, do not reject your mother's teaching: they will be a crown of grace for your head, a circlet for your neck."
Proverbs 1:8-9

"Do not be afraid, my child, if we have grown poor. You have great wealth if you fear God, if you shun every kind of sin and if you do what is pleasing to the Lord your God."
Tobit 4:23

"Listen to your father who begot you, do not despise your mother in her old age. [...] The father of the virtuous man will rejoice indeed, he who fathers a wise man will have joy of it. May you be the joy of your father, the gladness of her who bore you!"
Proverbs 23:22.24-25

"The same day, Tobit remembered the silver that he had left with Gabael at Rhages in Media and thought, 'I have come to the point of praying for death; I should do well to call my son Tobias and tell him about the money before I die.' He summoned his son Tobias and told him: 'When I die, give me an honorable burial. Honor your mother, and never abandon her all the days of your life. Do all that she wants, and give her no reason for sorrow. Remember, my child, all the risks she ran for your sake when you were in her womb. And when she dies, bury her at my side in the same grave.'" **Tobit 4:1-5**

"Children, be obedient to your parents in the Lord – that is your duty. The first commandment that has a promise attached to it is: Honor your father and mother, and the promise is: and you will prosper and have a long life in the land." **Ephesians 6:1-3**

"The lover of Wisdom makes his father glad, but the patron of harlots fritters his wealth away." **Proverbs 29:3**

"How can a youth remain pure? By behaving as your word prescribes." **Psalms 119[118]:9**

"You, too, my child, must prefer your own brothers; never presume to despise your brothers, the sons and daughters of your people; choose your wife from among them. For pride brings ruin and much worry; idleness causes need and poverty, for the mother of famine is idleness." **Tobit 4:13-14**

"Children, be obedient to your parents always, because that is what will please the Lord." **Colossians 3:20**

"The stick and the reprimand bestow wisdom, a child left to himself brings shame on his mother."
Proverbs 29:15

"My son, do not forget my teaching, let your heart keep my principles, for these will give you lengthier days, longer years of life, and greater happiness. Let kindliness and loyalty never leave you: tie them around your neck, write them on the tablet of your heart. So shall you enjoy favor and good repute in the sight of God and man."
Proverbs 3:1-4

"Do not be chary of correcting a child, a stroke of the cane is not likely to kill him. A stroke of the cane and you save him from Sheol."   **Proverbs 23:13-14**

"Your sons will all be taught by Yahweh. The prosperity of your sons will be great. You will be founded on integrity."
Isaiah 54:13-14a

"Long life comes to him who honors his father, he who sets his mother at ease is showing obedience to the Lord. He serves his parents as he does his Lord. Respect your father in deed as well as word, so that blessing may come on you from him."   **Ecclesiasticus 3:7-10**

"But Jesus said, 'Let the little children alone, and do not stop them coming to me; for it is to such as these that the kingdom of heaven belongs."   **Matthew 19:14**

"The crown of the aged is their children's children; the children's glory is their father."
Proverbs 17:6

"Children, listen to me your father, do what I tell you, and so be safe; for the Lord honors the father in his children, and upholds the rights of a mother over her sons Whoever respects his father is atoning for his sins."

Ecclesiasticus 3:1-3

"Honor your father and your mother, as Yahweh your God has commanded you, so that you may have long life and may prosper in the land that Yahweh your God gives to you."

Deuteronomy 5:16

"The first commandment that has a promise attached to it is: Honor your father and mother, and the promise is: and you will prosper and have a long life in the land."

Ephesians 6:2-3

"If a widow has children or grandchildren, they are to learn first of all to do their duty to their own families and repay their debt to their parents, because this is what pleases God."

I Timothy 5:4

Conjugal Problems

"Never have grudges against others, or lose your temper, or raise your voice to anybody, or call each other names, or allow any sort of spitefulness. Be friends with one another, and kind, forgiving each other as readily as God forgave you in Christ." **Ephesians 4:31-32**

"Love is the one thing that cannot hurt your neighbor; that is why it is the answer to every one of the commandments." **Romans 13:10**

"You have been obedient to the truth and purified your souls until you can love like brothers, in sincerity; let your love for each other be real and from the heart." **I Peter 1:22**

"Love each other as much as brothers should, and have a profound respect for each other. Work for the Lord with untiring effort and with great earnestness of spirit." **Romans 12:10-11**

"If you will not serve Yahweh, choose today whom you wish to serve, whether the gods that your ancestors served beyond the River, or the gods of the Amorites in whose land you are now living. As for me and my House, we will serve Yahweh." **Joshua 24:15**

"In the same way, wives should be obedient to their husbands. Then, if there are some husbands who have not yet obeyed the word, they may find themselves won over, without a word spoken, by the way their wives behave."

I Peter 3:1

"In the same way, husbands must always treat their wives with consideration in their life together, respecting a woman as one who, though she may be the weaker partner, is equally an heir to the life of grace. This will stop anything from coming in the way of your prayers."

I Peter 3:7

"And here is something else you do: you cover the altar of Yahweh with tears, with weeping and wailing, because he now refuses to consider the offering or to accept it from your hands. And you ask, 'Why?' It is because Yahweh stands as witness between you and the wife of your youth, the wife with whom you have broken faith, even though she was your partner and your wife by covenant. Did he not create a single being that has flesh and the breath of life? And what is this single being destined for? God-given offspring.

Be careful for your own life, therefore, and do not break faith with the wife of your youth. For I hate divorce, says Yahweh the God of Israel, and I hate people to parade their sins on their cloaks, says Yahweh Sabaoth. Respect your own life, therefore, and do not break faith like this."

Malachi 2:13-16

"You have learned how it was said: You must not commit adultery. But I say this to you: if a man looks at a woman lustfully, he has already committed adultery with her in his heart."   **Matthew 5:27-28**

"I give you a new commandment: love one another; just as I have loved you, you also must love one another. By this

194

love you have for one another, everyone will know that you are my disciples." **John 13:34-35**

"Even if you are angry, you must not sin: never let the sun set on your anger or else you will give the devil a foothold." **Ephesians 4:26-27**

"Never pay back one wrong with another, or an angry word with another one; instead, pay back with a blessing. That is what you are called to do, so that you inherit a blessing yourself. Remember: Anyone who wants to have a happy life and to enjoy prosperity must banish malice from his tongue, deceitful conversation from his lips; he must never yield to evil but must practice good; he must seek peace and pursue it. Because the face of the Lord frowns on evil men, but the eyes of the Lord are turned toward the virtuous, his ears to their cry." **I Peter 3:9-12**

"All you need say is 'Yes' if you mean yes, 'No' if you mean no; anything more than this comes from the evil one." **Matthew 5:37**

"You have learned how it was said: Eye for eye and tooth for tooth. But I say this to you: offer the wicked man no resistance. On the contrary, if anyone hits you on the right cheek, offer him the other as well." **Matthew 5:38-39**

"Be compassionate as your Father is compassionate. Do not judge, and you will not be judged yourselves; do not condemn, and you will not be condemned yourselves; grant pardon, and you will be pardoned." **Luke 6:36-37**

"Yes, if you forgive others their failings, your heavenly Father will forgive you yours; but if you do not forgive others, your Father will not forgive your failings either."

Matthew 6:14-15

"And when you stand in prayer, forgive whatever you have against anybody, so that your Father in heaven may forgive your failings too. But if you do not forgive, your Father in heaven will not forgive your failings either."

Mark 11:25-26

"Hatred provokes disputes, love covers over all offenses."

Proverbs 10:12

"Love is always patient and kind; it is never jealous; love is never boastful or conceited; it is never rude or selfish; it does not take offense, and is not resentful. Love takes no pleasure in other people's sins but delights in the truth; it is always ready to excuse, to trust, to hope, and to endure whatever comes."

I Corinthians 13:4-7

Separation and Divorce

"For the married I have something to say, and this is not from me but from the Lord: a wife must not leave her husband – or if she does leave him, she must either remain unmarried or else make it up with her husband – nor must a husband send his wife away.

The rest is from me and not from the Lord. If a brother has a wife who is an unbeliever, and she is content to live with him, he must not send her away; and if a woman has an unbeliever for her husband, and he is content to live with her, she must not leave him.

This is because the unbelieving husband is made one with the saints through his wife, and the unbelieving wife is made one with the saints through her husband. If this were not so, your children would be unclean, whereas in fact they are holy. However, if the unbelieving partner does not consent, they may separate; in these circumstances, the brother or sister is not tied: God has called you to a life of peace. If you are a wife, it may be your part to save your husband, for all you know; if a husband, for all you know, it may be your part to save your wife."

I Corinthians 7:10-16

"It has also been said: Anyone who divorces his wife must give her a writ of dismissal. But I say this to you: everyone who divorces his wife, except for the case of fornication, makes her an adulteress; and anyone who marries a divorced woman commits adultery."

Matthew 5:31-32

"So it is the man who consorts with his neighbor's wife: no one who touches her will go unpunished."

Proverbs 6:29

"Everyone who divorces his wife and marries another is guilty of adultery, and the man who marries a woman divorced by her husband commits adultery."

Luke 16:18

"Some Pharisees approached him and asked, 'Is it against the law for a man to divorce his wife?' They were testing him. He answered them, 'What did Moses command you?' 'Moses allowed us,' they said, 'to draw up a writ of dismissal and so to divorce.' Then Jesus said to them, 'It was because you were so unteachable that he wrote this commandment for you. But from the beginning of creation God made them male and female. This is why a man must leave father and mother, and the two become one body. They are no longer two, therefore, but one body. So then, what God has united, man must not divide.' Back in the house the disciples questioned him again about this, and he said to them, 'The man who divorces his wife and marries another is guilty of adultery against her. And if a woman divorces her husband and marries another she is guilty of adultery too.'"

Mark 10:2-12

"And here is something else you do: you cover the altar of Yahweh with tears, with weeping and wailing, because he now refuses to consider the offering or to accept it from your hands. And you ask, 'Why?' It is because Yahweh stands as witness between you and the wife of your youth, the wife with whom you have broken faith, even though she was your

198

partner and your wife by covenant. Did he not create a single being that has flesh and the breath of life? And what is this single being destined for? God-given offspring. Be careful for your own life, therefore, and do not break faith with the wife of your youth." **Malachi 2:13-15**

"Take no notice of a loose-living woman, for the lips of this alien drip with honey, her words are smoother than oil, but their outcome is bitter as wormwood, sharp as a two-edged sword. [...] And now, my son, listen to me, never deviate from what I say: set your course as far from her as possible, go nowhere near the foor of her house, or you will surrender your honor to others, your years to one who has no pity, and strangers will batten on your property, your labors going to some alien house." **Proverbs 5:3-4.7-10**

"Why be seduced, my son, by an alien woman, and fondle the breast of a woman who is a stranger? For the eyes of Yahweh observe a man's ways and survey all his paths. The wicked man is snared in his own misdeeds, is caught in the meshes of his own sin." **Proverbs 5:20-22**

Widowhood

"A wife is tied as long as her husband is alive. But if the husband dies, she is free to marry anybody she likes, only it must be in the Lord. She would be happier, in my opinion, if she stayed as she is – and I too have the Spirit of God, I think." **I Corinthians 7:39-40**

"Sing to Yahweh, play music to his name, build a road for the Rider of the Clouds, rejoice in Yahweh, exult at his coming! Father of orphans, defender of widows, such is God in his holy dwelling." **Psalms 68[67]:4-5**

"I think it is best for young widows to marry again and have children and a home to look after, and not give the enemy any chance to raise a scandal about them [...]. If a Christian woman has widowed relatives, she should support them and not make the Church bear the expense but enable it to support those who are genuinely widows." **I Timothy 5:14.16**

"Pure, unspoiled religion, in the eyes of God our Father is this: coming to the help of orphans and widows when they need it, and keeping oneself uncontaminated by the world." **James 1:27**

"A curse on him who tampers with the rights of the stranger, the orphan and the widow." **Deuteronomy 27:19a**

"Be considerate to widows; I mean those who are truly widows. If a widow has children or grandchildren, they are to learn first of all to do their duty to their own families and repay their debt to their parents, because this is what pleases God.

But a woman who is really widowed and left without anybody can give herself up to God and consecrate all her days and nights to petitions and prayer. The one who thinks only of pleasure is already dead while she is still alive: remind them of all this, too, so that their lives may be blameless."

I Timothy 5:3-7

"There is something I want to add for the sake of widows and those who are not married: it is a good thing for them to stay as they are, like me, but if they cannot control the sexual urges, they should get married, since it is better to be married than to be tortured."   **I Corinthians 7:8-9**

"For now your creator will be your husband, his name, Yahweh Sabaoth; your redeemer will be the Holy One of Israel, he is called the God of the whole earth."

Isaiah 54:5

"Yahweh protects the stranger, he keeps the orphan and widow, and frustrates the wicked."   **Psalms 146[145]:9**

"It is he who sees justice done for the orphan and the widow, who loves the stranger and gives him food and clothing."   **Deuteronomy 10:18**

"Yahweh pulls down the house of the proud, but he keeps the widow's boundaries intact."   **Proverbs 15:25**

"Do not oppress the widow and the orphan, the settler and the poor man, and do not secretly plan evil against one another."   **Zechariah 7:10**

201

"A woman in childbirth suffers, because her time has come; but when she has given birth to the child she forgets the suffering in her joy that a man has been born into the world. So it is with you: you are sad now, but I shall see you again, and your hearts will be full of joy, and that joy no one shall take from you."   **John 16:21-22**

"And teach them to observe all the commands I gave you. And know that I am with you always; yes, to the end of time."   **Matthew 28:20**

"Do not be afraid, you will not be put to shame, do not be dismayed, you will not be disgraced; for you will forget the shame of your youth and no longer remember the curse of your widowhood. For now your creator will be your husband, his name, Yahweh Sabaoth; your redeemer will be the Holy One of Israel, he is called the God of the whole earth. Yes, like a forsaken wife, distressed in spirit, Yahweh calls you back. Does a man cast off the wife of his youth? says your God.

[...] For the mountains may depart, the hills be shaken, but my love for you will never leave you and my covenant of peace with you will never be shaken, says Yahweh who takes pity on you."   **Isaiah 54:4-6.10**

Maturity and Old Age

"In you, Yahweh, I take shelter; never let me be disgraced. In your righteousness rescue me, deliver me, turn your ear to me and save me! Be a sheltering rock for me, a walled fortress to save me! For you are my rock, my fortress.

My God, rescue me from the hands of the wicked, from the clutches of rogue and tyrant!

For you alone are my hope, Lord, Yahweh, I have trusted you since my youth, I have relied on you since I was born, you have been my portion from my mother's womb, and the constant theme of my praise.

[...] Do not reject me now I am old, nor desert me now my strength is failing. [...] God, you taught me when I was young, and I am still proclaiming your marvels. Now that I am old and gray, God, do not desert me; let me live to tell the rising generation about your strength and power, about your heavenly righteousness, God. You have done great things; who, God, is comparable to you?"

Psalms 71[70]:1-6.9.17-19

"I rescue all who cling to me, I protect whoever knows my name, I answer everyone who invokes me, I am with them when they are in trouble; I bring them safety and honor. I give them life, long and full, and show them how I can save."

Psalms 91[90]:14-16

"In your old age I shall be still the same, when your hair is gray I shall still support you. I have already done so, I have carried you, I shall still support and deliver you."

Isaiah 46:4

"White hairs are a crown of honor, they are found in the paths of virtue." **Proverbs 16:31**

"So the virtuous flourish like palm trees [...]. Planted in the house of Yahweh, they will flourish in the courts of our God, Still bearing fruit in old age, still remaining fresh and green, to proclaim that Yahweh is righteous, my rock in whom no fault is to be found!" **Psalms 92[91]:12a.13-15**

"My son, do not forget my teaching, let your heart keep my principles, for these will give you lengthier days, longer years of life, and greater happiness." **Proverbs 3:1-2**

"Happy the man who discovers wisdom [...]. In her right hand is length of days; in her left hand, riches and honor." **Proverbs 3:13a.16**

"Ah, how goodness and kindness pursue me, every day of my life; my home, the house of Yahweh, as long as I live!" **Psalms 23[22]:6**

"Now I am old, but ever since my youth I never saw a virtuous man deserted, or his descendants forced to beg their bread." **Psalms 37[36]:25**

"Put greed out of your lives and be content with whatever you have; God himself has said: I will not fail you or desert you." **Hebrews 13:5**

"Yahweh guards you from harm, he guards your lives, he guards you leaving, coming back, now and for always." **Psalms 121[120]:7-8**

"Follow the whole way that Yahweh has marked for you and you shall live, you shall prosper and shall live long in the land you are to possess."   **Deuteronomy 5:33**

"I keep Yahweh before me always, for with him at my right hand nothing can shake me."

Psalms 16[15]:8

"You shall see your descendants multiply, your offspring grow like the grass in the fields. In ripe age you shall go to the grave, like a wheat sheaf stacked in due season."

Job 5:25-26

"The fear of Yahweh is the beginning of wisdom; the knowledge of the Holy One – perception indeed! For days are multiplied by me and years of life increased."

Proverbs 9:10-11

3

Promises of God for Spiritual Growth

In the Faith

"Now it is impossible to please God without faith, since anyone who comes to him must believe that he exists and rewards those who try to find him."

Hebrews 11:6

"Only faith can guarantee the blessings that we hope for, or prove the existence of the realities that at present remain unseen."   **Hebrews 11:1**

"And his commandments are not difficult, because anyone who has been begotten by God has already overcome the world; this is the victory over the world – our faith."

I John 5:4

"That is why what fulfills the promise depends on faith, so that it may be a free gift and be available to all of Abraham's descendants, not only those who belong to the Law but also those who belong to the faith of Abraham who is the father of all of us."   **Romans 4:16**

"This is a cause of great joy for you, even though you may for a short time have to bear being plagued by all sorts of trials; so that, when Jesus Christ is revealed, your faith will have been tested and proved like gold – only it is more precious than gold, which is corruptible even though it bears testing by fire – and then you will have praise and glory and honor.

You did not see him, yet you love him; and still without seeing him, you are already filled with a joy so glorious that it cannot be described, because you believe; and you are sure of the end to which your faith looks forward, that is, the salvation of your souls."   **I Peter 1:6-9**

"So far then we have seen that, through our Lord Jesus Christ, by faith we are judged righteous and at peace with God, since it is by faith and through Jesus that we have entered this state of grace in which we can boast about looking forward to God's glory."   **Romans 5:1-2**

"So faith comes from what is preached, and what is preached comes from the word of Christ."
                                        Romans 10:17

"Since this is what reveals the justice of God to us: it shows how faith leads to faith, or as scripture says: The upright man finds life throuth faith."   **Romans 1:17**

"The Law will not justify anyone in the sight of God, because we are told: the righteous man finds life through faith."   **Galatians 3:11**

"Jesus answered, 'Have faith in God. I tell you solemnly, if anyone says to this mountain,' 'Get up and throw yourself into the sea,' with no hesitation in his heart but believing that what he says will happen, it will be done for him. I tell you therefore: everything you ask and pray for, believe that you have it already, and it will be yours."
                          Mark 11:22-24

"You and I are not the sort of people who draw back, and are lost by it; we are the sort who keep faithful until our souls are saved."   **Hebrews 10:39**

"If one of you is ill, he should send for the elders of the church, and they must anoint him with oil in the name of the Lord and pray over him. The prayer of faith will save the sick man and the Lord will raise him up again; and if he has committed any sins, he will be forgiven."
                          James 5:14-15

"Then from behind him came a woman, who had suffered from a hemorrhage for twelve years, and she touched the fringe of his cloak, for she said to herself, 'If I can only touch his cloak I shall be well again.' Jesus turned around and saw her and he said to her, 'Courage, my daughter, your faith has restored you to health.' And from that moment the woman was well again."
                          Matthew 9:20-22

"You understand that your faith is only put to the test to make you patient."   **James 1:3**

"And you are, all of you, sons of God through faith in Christ Jesus."   **Galatians 3:26**

"And when Jesus reached the house the blind men came up with him and he said to them, 'Do you believe I can do this?' They said , 'Sir, we do.' Then he touched their eyes saying, 'Your faith deserves it, so let this be done for you.'"   **Matthew 9:28-29**

"Christians are told by the Spirit to look to faith for those rewards that righteousness hopes for, since in Christ Jesus whether you are circumcised or not makes no difference – what matters is faith that makes its power felt through love."   **Galatians 5:5-6**

"'If you can?' retorted Jesus. 'Everything is possible for anyone who has faith.'"   **Mark 9:23**

"Because it is by grace that you have been saved, through faith; not by anything of your own, but by a gift from God."   **Ephesians 2:8**

"In the light of the grace I have received I want to urge each one among you not to exaggerate his real importance. Each of you must judge himself soberly by the standard of the faith God has given him."   **Romans 12:3**

"Our one desire is that [...] never growing careless, but imitating those who have the faith and the perseverance to inherit the promises."   **Hebrews 6:11a.12**

"The Lord is faithful, and he will give you strength and guard you from the evil one."   **II Thessalonians 3:3**

"So as we go in, let us be sincere in heart and filled with faith, our minds sprinkled and free from any trace of bad conscience and our bodies washed with pure water."

Hebrews 10:22

"He answered, 'Because you have little faith. I tell you solemnly, if your faith were the size of a mustard seed you could say to this mountain, 'Move from here to there,' and it would move; nothing would be impossible for you. As for this kind (of devil), it is cast out only by prayer and fasting."

Matthew 17:20-21

"Take the case, my brothers, of someone who has never done a single good act but claims that he has faith. Will that faith save him? If one of the brothers or one of the sisters is in need of clothes and has not enough food to live on, and one of you says to them, 'I wish you well; keep yourself warm and eat plenty,' without giving them these bare necessities of life, then what good is that? Faith is like that: if good works do not go with it, it is quite dead. [...] A body dies when it is separated from the spirit, and in the same way faith is dead if it is separated from good deeds."

James 2:14-17.26

"Listen, my dear brothers: it was those who are poor according to the world that God chose, to be rich in faith and to be the heirs to the kingdom which he promised to those who love him." **James 2:5**

"Going as we do by faith and not by sight."

II Corinthians 5:7

"Through him you now have faith in God, who raised him from the dead and gave him glory for that very reason – so that you would have faith and hope in God."

I Peter 1:21

"Do not let your hearts be troubled. Trust in God still, and trust in me."   **John 14:1**

"So that Christ may live in your hearts through faith, and then, planted in love and built on love, you will with all the saints have strength to grasp the breadth and the length, the height and the depth; until, knowing the love of Christ, which is beyond all knowledge, you are filled with the utter fullness of God."   **Ephesians 3:17-19**

In the Love of God

"This is the love I mean: not our love for God, but God's love for us when he sent his Son to be the sacrifice that takes our sins away. [...] We ourselves have known and put our faith in God's love toward ourselves. God is love and anyone who lives in love lives in God, and God lives in him. [...] We are to love, then, because he loved us first."

I John 4:10.16.19

"Jesus replied, 'This is the first: Listen, Israel, the Lord our God is the one Lord, and you must love the Lord your God with all your heart, with all your soul, with all your mind and with all your strength. The second is this: You must love your neighbor as yourself. There is no commandment greater than these."

Mark 12:29-31

"Because the Father himself loves you for loving me and believing that I came from God."

John 16:27

"As the Father has loved me, so I have loved you. Remain in my love. If you keep my commandments you will remain in my love, just as I have kept my Father's commandments and remain in his love. [...] You are my friends, if you do what I command you." **John 15:9-10.14**

"Anybody who receives my commandments and keeps them will be one who loves me; and anybody who loves me will be loved by my Father, and I shall love him and show myself to him." **John 14:21**

"Jesus replied: 'If anyone loves me he will keep my word, and my Father will love him, and we shall come to him and make our home with him. Those who do not love me do not keep my words. And my word is not my own: it is the word of the one who sent me." **John 14:23-24**

"This is what loving God is – keeping his commandments; and his commandments are not difficult."
I John 5:3-4a

"We teach scripture calls: the things that no eye has seen and no ear has heard, things beyond the mind of man, all that God has prepared for those who love him."
I Corinthians 2:9

"Know then that Yahweh your God is God indeed, the faithful God who is true to his covenant and his graciousness for a thousand generations toward those who love him and keep his commandments." **Deuteronomy 7:9**

"Keep yourselves within the love of God and wait for the mercy of our Lord Jesus Christ to give you eternal life."
Jude 21

"We know that by turning everything to their good God co-operates with all those who love him, with all those that he has called according to his purpose."
Romans 8:28

"But any man who loves God is known by him."
I Corinthians 8:3

"And I said, 'Yahweh, God of heaven, great God who must be feared, maintaining covenant and kindness with those who love you and obey your commandments."
Nehemiah 1:5

"I show kindness to thousands of those who love me and keep my commandments."   **Exodus 20:6**

"Under his protection the pious are safe, but Yahweh is destruction to the wicked."   **Psalms 145[144]:20**

In the Love for One's Neighbor

"Do not let your love be a pretense, but sincerely prefer good to evil. [...] If any of the saints are in need you must share with them; and you should make hospitality your special care."   **Romans 12:9.13**

"If I have all the eloquence of men or of angels, but speak without love, I am simply a gong booming or a cymbal clashing. If I have the gift of prophecy, understanding all the mysteries there are, and knowing everything, and if I have faith in all its fullness, to move mountains, but without love, then I am nothing at all. If I give away all that I possess, piece by piece, and if I even let them take my body to burn it, but am without love, it will do me no good whatever.

Love is always patient and kind; it is never jealous; love is never boastful or conceited; it is never rude or selfish; it does not take offense, and is not resentful. Love takes no pleasure in other people's sins but delights in the truth; it is always ready to excuse, to trust, to hope, and to endure whatever comes. Love does not come to an end."

I Corinthians 13:1-8a

"I say this to you: love your enemies and pray for those who persecute you."   **Matthew 5:44**

"If you love those who love you, what thanks can you expect? Even sinners love those who love them. And if you do good to those who do good to you, what thanks can you expect? For even sinners do that much. And if you lend to those from whom you hope to receive, what thanks can you expect?

Even sinners lend to sinners to get back the same amount. Instead, love your enemies and do good, and lend without any hope of return. You will have a great reward, and you will be sons of the Most High, for he himself is kind to the ungrateful and the wicked." **Luke 6:32-35**

"I give you a new commandment: love one another; just as I have loved you, you also must love one another. By this love you have for one another, everyone will know that you are my disciples." **John 13:34-35**

"This is my commandment: love one another, as I have loved you. A man can have no greater love than to lay down his life for his friends." **John 15:12-13**

"Anyone who loves his brother is living in the light and need not be afraid of stumbling." **I John 2:10**

"We have passed out of death and into life, and of this we can be sure because we love our brothers. If you refuse to love, you must remain dead." **I John 3:14-15a**

"My children, our love is not to be just words or mere talk, but something real and active."

I John 3:18

"My dear people, let us love one another since love comes from God and everyone who loves is begotten by God and knows God. Anyone who fails to love can never have known God, because God is love." **I John 4:7-8**

"So this is the commandment that he has given us, that anyone who loves God must also love his brother."

I John 4:21

"We can be sure that we love God's children if we love God himself and do what he has commanded us."
I John 5:2

"Never repay evil with evil but let everyone see that you are interested only in the highest ideals. Do all you can to live at peace with everyone. Never try to get revenge; leave that, my friends, to God's anger. As scripture says: Vengeance is mine – I will pay them back, the Lord promises. But there is more: If your enemy is hungry, you should give him food, and if he is thirsty, let him drink. Thus you heap red-hot coals on his head. Resist evil and conquer it with good."
Romans 12:17-21

"You have been obedient to the truth and purified your souls until you can love like brothers, in sincerity; let your love for each other be real and from the heart."
I Peter 1:22

"Finally: you should all agree among yourselves and be sympathetic; love the brothers, have compassion and be self-effacing. Never pay back one wrong with another, or an angry word with another one; instead, pay back with a blessing. That is what you are called to do, so that you inherit a blessing yourself." **I Peter 3:8-9**

"Bear with one another; forgive each other as soon as a quarrel begins. The Lord has forgiven you; now you must do the same. Over all these clothes, to keep them together and complete them, put on love." **Colossians 3:13-14**

"So always treat others as you would like them to treat you; that is the meaning of the Law and the Prophets."
Matthew 7:12

"Avoid getting into debt, except the debt of mutual love. If you love your fellow men you have carried out your obligations. All the commandments: You shall not commit adultery, you shall not kill, you shall not steal, you shall not covet, and so on, are summed up in this single command: You must love your neighbor as yourself. Love is the one thing that cannot hurt your neighbor; that is why it is the answer to every one of the commandments."

Romans 13:8-10

"I, the prisioner in the Lord, implore you therefore to lead a life worthy of your vocation. Bear with one another charitably, in complete selflessness, gentleness and patience." **Ephesians 4:1-2**

"If a man who was rich enough in this world's goods saw that one of his brothers was in need, but closed his heart to him, how could the love of God be living in him? My children, our love is not to be just words or mere talk, but something real and active; only by this can we be certain that we are children of the truth and be able to quiet our conscience in his presence." **I John 3:17-19**

"Try, then, to imitate God, as children of his that he loves, and follow Christ by loving as he loved you, giving himself up in our place as a fragrant offering and a sacrifice to God." **Ephesians 5:1-2**

In Forgiveness

"If your brother does something wrong, go and have it out with him alone, between your two selves. If he listens to you, you have won back your brother. If he does not listen, take one or two others along with you: the evidence of two or three witnesses is required to sustain any charge. But if he refuses to listen to these, report it to the community; and if he refuses to listen to the community, treat him like a pagan or a tax collector. I tell you solemnly, whatever you bind on earth shall be considered bound in heaven; whatever you loose on earth shall be considered loosed in heaven."

Matthew 18:15-18

"Never pay back one wrong with another, or an angry word with another one; instead, pay back with a blessing. That is what you are called to do, so that you inherit a blessing yourself. Remember: Anyone who wants to have a happy life and to enjoy prosperity must banish malice from his tongue, deceitful conversation from his lips."

I Peter 3:9-10

"Yes, if you forgive others their failings, your heavenly Father will forgive you yours; but if you do not forgive others, your Father will not forgive your failings either."

Matthew 6:14-15

"Bear with one another; forgive each other as soon as a quarrel begins. The Lord has forgiven you; now you must do the same." **Colossians 3:13**

"But I say this to you: love your enemies and pray for those who persecute you; in this way you will be sons of your

Father in heaven, for he causes his sun to rise on bad men as well as good, and his rain to fall on honest and dishonest men alike." **Matthew 5:44-45**

"Instead, love your enemies and do good, and lend without any hope of return. You will have a great reward, and you will be sons of the Most High, for he himself is kind to the ungrateful and the wicked. [...] Do not judge, and you will not be judged yourselves; do not condemn, and you will not be condemned yourselves; grant pardon, and you will be pardoned." **Luke 6:35.37**

"If your brother does something wrong, reprove him and, if he is sorry, forgive him." **Luke 17:3b**

"Do not say, 'I will repay evil'; put your hope in Yahweh and he will keep you safe." **Proverbs 20:22**

"He who exacts vengeance will experience the vengeance of the Lord, who keeps strict account of sin. Forgive your neighbor the hurt he does you, and when you pray, your sins will be forgiven. If a man nurses anger against another, can he then demand compassion from the Lord? Showing no pity for a man like himself, can he then plead for his own sins? Mere creature of flesh, he cherishes resentment; who will forgive him his sins?

Remember the last things, and stop hating, remember dissolution and death, and live by the commandments. Remember the commandments, and do not bear your neighbor ill will; remember the covenant of the Most High, and overlook the offense." **Ecclesiasticus 28:1-9**

221

"And when you stand in prayer, forgive whatever you have against anybody, so that your Father in heaven may forgive your failings too."   **Mark 11:25**

"You see, there is some merit in putting up with the pains of unearned punishment if it is done for the sake of God but there is nothing meritorious in taking a beating patiently if you have done something wrong to deserve it. The merit, in the sight of God, is in bearing it patiently when you are punished after doing your duty. This, in fact, is what you were called to do, because Christ suffered for you and left an example for you to follow the way he took."
I Peter 2:19-21

"Happy those who are persecuted in the cause of right: theirs is the kingdom of heaven. Happy are you when people abuse you and persecute you and speak all kinds of calumny against you on my account. Rejoice and be glad, for your reward will be great in heaven; this is how they persecuted the prophets before you."   **Matthew 5:10-12**

"Then Peter went up to him and said, 'Lord, how often must I forgive my brother if he wrongs me? As often as seven times?' Jesus answered, 'Not seven, I tell you, but seventy-seven times.'"   **Matthew 18:21-22**

"It is a blessing for you when they insult you for bearing the name of Christ, because it means that you have the Spirit of glory, the Spirit of God resting on you."
I Peter 4:14

"Never have grudges against others, or lose your temper, or raise your voice to anybody, or call each other names, or allow any sort of spitefulness. Be friends with one another, and kind, forgiving each other as readily as God forgave you in Christ." **Ephesians 4:31-32**

"If your enemy is hungry, you should give him food, and if he is thirsty, let him drink. Thus you heap red-hot coals on his head. Resist evil and conquer it with good." **Romans 12:20b-21**

In Joy

"He then said, '[Do not be sad: the joy of Yahweh is your stronghold.'" **Nehemiah 8:10**

"I will exult, and rejoice in your love! You, who have seen my wretchedness, and known the miseries of my soul." **Psalms 31[30]:7**

"Light dawns for the virtuous, and joy, for upright hearts." **Psalms 97[96]:11**

"The fear of the Lord is glory and pride, and happiness and a crown of joyfulness. The fear of the Lord will gladden the heart, giving happiness and joy and long life." **Ecclesiasticus 1:11-12**

"My son, from your earliest youth choose instruction, and till your hair is white you will keep finding wisdom. [...] For in the end you will find rest in her and she will take the form of joy for you." **Ecclesiasticus 6:18.29**

"Through it will run a highway undefiled [...] for those Yahweh has ransomed shall return. They will come to Zion shouting for joy, everlasting joy on their faces; joy and gladness will go with them and sorrow and lament be ended." **Isaiah 35:8a.10**

"Yes, Yahweh has pity on Zion, has pity on all her ruins; turns her desolation into an Eden, her wasteland into the garden of Yahweh. Joy and gladness shall be found in her, thanksgiving and the sound of music."

Isaiah 51:3

"For their shame was twofold, disgrace and spitting their lot. Twofold therefore shall they possess in their land, everlasting joy is theirs." **Isaiah 61:7**

"She fills their whole house with their heart's desire. The fear of the Lord is the crown of wisdom."

Eclesiasticus 1:17-18

"I keep Yahweh before me always, for with him at my right hand nothing can shake me. So my heart exults, my very soul rejoices, my body, too, will rest securely."

Psalms 16[15]:8-9

"Let God arise, let his enemies be scattered, let those who hate him flee before him! As smoke disperses, they disperse; as wax melts when near the fire, so the wicked perish when God approaches. But at God's approach, the virtuous rejoice, exulting and singing for joy."

Psalms 68[67]:1-3

"But I will rejoice in Yahweh, I will exult in God my savior." **Habakkuk 3:18**

"Your word was my delight and the joy of my heart; for I was called by your name, Yahweh, God of Sabaoth."

Jeremiah 15:16b

"For now I create new heavens and a new earth, and the past will not be remembered, and will come no more to men's minds. Be glad and rejoice for ever and ever for what I am creating, because I now create Jerusalem 'Joy' and her people 'Gladness.' I shall rejoice over Jerusalem and exult in my people. No more will the sound of weeping or the sound of cries be heard in her."   **Isaiah 65:17-19**

"Like a son comforted by his mother will I comfort you. (And by Jerusalem you will be comforted.) At the sight your will rejoice, and your bones flourish like the grass. To his servants Yahweh will reveal his hand, but to his enemies his fury."   **Isaiah 66:13-14**

"When that day comes, word will come to Jerusalem: [...] Yahweh your God is in your midst, a victorious warrior. He will exult with joy over you, he will renew you by his love; he will dance with shouts of joy for you as on a day of festival. I have taken away your misfortune, no longer need you bear the disgrace of it."   **Zephaniah 3:16a.17-18**

"Do not torment yourself with brooding. Gladness of heart is life to a man, joy is what gives him length of days. Beguile your cares, console your heart, chase sorrow far away; for sorrow has been the ruin of many, and is no use to anybody. Jealousy and anger shorten your days, and worry brings premature old age."   **Ecclesiasticus 30:22-25**

"But the angel said, 'Do not be afraid. Listen, I bring you news of great joy, a joy to be shared by the whole people. Today in the town of David a savior has been born to you; he is Christ the Lord.'"   **Luke 2:10-11**

"And Mary said: 'My soul proclaims the greatness of the Lord and my spirit exults in God my savior; because he has looked upon his lowly handmaid. Yes, from this day forward all generations will call me blessed.'"

Luke 1:46-48

"The seventy-two came back rejoicing. 'Lord,' they said, 'even the devils submit to us when we use your name.' He said to them, 'I watched Satan fall like lightning from heaven. Yes, I have given you power to tread underfoot serpents and scorpions and the whole strength of the enemy; nothing shall ever hurt you. Yet do not rejoice that the Spirits submit to you; rejoice rather that your names are written in heaven.'"

Luke 10:17-18a.19-20

"I tell you most solemnly, you will be weeping and wailing while the world will rejoice; you will be sorrowful, but your sorrow will turn to joy. A woman in childbirth suffers, because her time has come; but when she has given birth to the child she forgets the suffering in her joy that a man has been born into the world. So it is with you: you are sad now, but I shall see you again, and your hearts will be full of joy, and that joy no one shall take from you." **John 16:20-22**

"If you keep my commandments you will remain in my love, just as I have kept my Father's commandments and remain in his love. I have told you this so that my own joy may be in you and your joy be complete."

John 15:10-11

"I tell you most solemnly: [...] Until now you have not asked for anything in my name. Ask and you will receive, and so your joy will be complete." **John 16:23b.24**

"Because the kingdom of God does not mean eating or drinking this or that, it means righteousness and peace and joy brought by the Holy Spirit."   **Romans 14:17**

"Let me put it like this: if you are guided by the Spirit you will be in no danger of yielding to self-indulgence. [...] What the Spirit brings is very different: love, joy, peace, patience, kindness, goodness, trustfulness, gentleness and self-control."   **Galatians 5:16.22-23a**

In Hope

"For the needy is not always forgotten, the hope of the poor is never brought to nothing." **Psalms 9:18**

"Happy the man who has the God of Jacob to help him, whose hope is fixed on Yahweh his God."
Psalms 146[145]:5

"Do not let your heart be envious of sinners but be steady every day in the fear of Yahweh; for there is a morrow, and your hope will not be nullified." **Proverbs 23:17-18**

"And such is knowledge of wisdom for your soul: find it, and there will be a morrow, and your hope will not be in vain." **Proverbs 24:14**

"Yes, the hope of the godless is like chaff carried on the wind, like fine spray driven by the gale; it disperses like smoke before the wind, goes like the memory of a one-day guest. But the virtuous live for ever, their recompense lies with the Lord, the Most High takes care of them. So they shall receive the royal crown of splendor, the diadem of beauty from the hand of the Lord; for he will shelter them with his right hand and shield them with his arm."
Wisdom 5:14-16

"But, disposing of such strength, you are mild in judgment, you govern us with great lenience, for you have only to will, and your power is there. By acting thus you have taught a lesson to your people how the virtuous man

must be kindly to his fellow men, and you have given your sons the good hope that after sin you will grant repentance."
Wisdom 12:18-19

"Happy the man whose own soul does not accuse him, and who has never given up hope." **Ecclesiasticus 14:2**

"Happy the rich man who is found to be blameless and does not go chasing after gold." **Ecclesiasticus 31:8**

"The man who fears the Lord will not be fainthearted, will not be daunted since the Lord is his hope."
Ecclesiasticus 34:16

"A blessing on the man who puts his trust in Yahweh, with Yahweh for his hope." **Jeremiah 17:7**

"And I hold the same hope in God as they do that there will be a resurrection of good men and bad men alike. In these things, I, as much as they, do my best to keep a clear conscience at all times before God and man."
Acts 24:15-16

"So far then we have seen that, through our Lord Jesus Christ, by faith we are judged righteous and at peace with God, since it is by faith and through Jesus that we have entered this state of grace in which we can boast about looking forward to God's glory. But that is not all we can boast about; we can boast about our sufferings. These sufferings bring patience, as we know, and patience brings perseverance, and perseverance brings hope, and this hope

is not deceptive, because the love of God has been poured into our hearts by the Holy Spirit which has been given us."
Romans 5:1-5

"And not only creation, but all of us who possess the first fruits of the Spirit, we too groan inwardly as we wait for our bodies to be set free. For we must be content to hope that we shall be saved – our salvation is not in sight, we should not have to be hoping for it if it were – but, as I say, we must hope to be saved since we are not saved yet – it is something we must wait for with patience." **Romans 8:23-25**

"It was not because he was concerned with any righteous actions we might have done ourselves; it was for no reason except his own compassion that he saved us, by means of the cleansing water of rebirth and by renewing us with the Holy Spirit. Which he has so generously poured over us through Jesus Christ our Savior. He did this so that we should be justified by his grace, to become heirs looking forward to inheriting eternal life." **Titus 3:5-7**

"But Christ was faithful as a son, and as the master in the house. And we are his house, as long as we cling to our hope with the confidence that we glory in."
Hebrews 3:6

"Let us keep firm in the hope we profess, because the one who made the promise is faithful."
Hebrews 10:23

"Blessed be God the Father of our Lord Jesus Christ, who in his great mercy has given us a new birth as his sons, by raising Jesus Christ from the dead, so that we have a sure hope and the promise of an inheritance that can never be spoiled or soiled and never fade away, because it is being kept for you in the heavens."   **I Peter 1:3-4**

"Through him you now have faith in God, who raised him from the dead and gave him glory for that very reason – so that you would have faith and hope in God."
                                                        I Peter 1:21

"Always have your answer ready for people who ask you the reason for the hope that you all have. But give it with courtesy and respect and with a clear conscience, so that those who slander you when you are living a good life in Christ may be proved wrong in the accusations that they bring."   **I Peter 3:15c-16**

"My dear people, we are already the children of God but what we are to be in the future has not yet been revealed; all we know is, that when it is revealed we shall be like him because we shall see him as he really is. Surely everyone who entertains this hope must purify himself, must try to be as pure as Christ."   **I John 3:2-3**

"In the same way, when God wanted to make the heirs to the promise thoroughly realize that his purpose was unalterable, he conveyed this by an oath; so that there would be two unalterable things in which it was impossible for God to be lying, and so that we, now we have found safety, should have a strong encouragement to take a firm grip on the hope that is held out to us. Here we have an anchor for our soul, as sure as it is firm, and reaching right through beyond the veil where Jesus has entered before us and on our behalf, to become a high priest of the order of Melchizedek, and for ever." **Hebrews 6:17-20**

"We know that by turning everything to their good God co-operates with all those who love him, with all those that he has called according to his purpose."

Romans 8:28

In Devotion

"Physical exercises are useful enough, but the usefulness of spirituality is unlimited, since it holds out the reward of life here and now and of the future life as well."
I Timothy 4:8

"Religion, of course, does bring large profits, but only to those who are content with they have."
I Timothy 6:6

"But, as a man dedicated to God, you must avoid all that. You must aim to be saintly and religious, filled with faith and love, patient and gentle."
I Timothy 6:11

"You are well aware, then, that anybody who tries to live in devotion to Christ is certain to be attacked."
II Timothy 3:12

"And taught us that what we have to do is to give up everything that does not lead to God, and all our worldly ambitions; we must be self-restrained and live good and religious lives here in this present world, while we are waiting in hope for the blessing which will come with the Appearing of the glory of our great God and Savior Christ Jesus."
Titus 2:12-13

"By his divine power, he has given us all the things that we need for life and for true devotion, bringing us to know God himself, who has called us by his own glory and goodness. In making these gifts, he has given us the guarantee of something very great and wonderful to come: through them you will be able to share the divine nature and to escape corruption in a world that is sunk in vice. But to attain this, you will have to do your utmost yourselves, adding goodness to the faith that you have, understanding to your goodness, self-control to your understanding, patience to your self-control, true devotion to your patience, kindness toward your fellow men to your devotion, and, to this kindness, love. If you have a generous supply of these, they will not leave you ineffectual or unproductive: they will bring you to a real knowledge of our Lord Jesus Christ."

II Peter 1:3-8

"Since everything is coming to an end like this, you should be living holy and saintly lives while you wait and long for the Day of God to come, when the sky will dissolve in flames and the elements melt in the heat. What we are waiting for is what he promised: the new heavens and new earth, the place where righteousness will be at home."

II Peter 3:11-13

In Prayer

"Long before they call I shall answer; before they stop speaking I shall have heard."   **Isaiah 65:24**

"Call to me and I will answer you; I will tell you great mysteries of which you know nothing."
Jeremiah 33:3

"For my part, I look to Yahweh, my hope is in the God who will save me; my God will hear me."
Micah 7:7

"I love! For Yahweh listens to my entreaty; he bends down to listen to me when I call." **Psalms 116[114]:1-2**

"The Spirit too comes to help us in our weakness. For when we cannot choose words in order to pray properly, the Spirit himself expresses our plea in a way that could never be put into words."   **Romans 8:26**

"But when you pray, go to your private room and, when you have shut your door, pray to your Father who is in that secret place, and your Father who sees all that is done in secret will reward you."   **Matthew 6:6**

"I tell you therefore: everything you ask and pray for, believe that you have it already, and it will be yours. And when you stand in prayer, forgive whatever you have against anybody, so that your Father in heaven may forgive your failings too.

But if you do not forgive, your Father in heaven will not forgive your failings either." **Mark 11:24-26**

"Yahweh stands far from the wicked, but he listens to the prayers of the virtuous." **Proverbs 15:29**

"And indeed, what great nation is there that has its gods so near as Yahweh our God is to us whenever we call to him?" **Deuteronomy 4:7**

"Lord, you are good and forgiving, most loving to all who invoke you; Yahweh, hear my prayer, listen to me as I plead. Lord, in trouble I invoke you, and you answer my prayer." **Psalms 86[85]:5.7**

"The nearer you go to God, the nearer he will come to you. Clean your hands, you sinners, and clear your minds, you waverers." **James 4:8**

"I, for myself, appeal to God and Yahweh saves me." **Psalms 55[54]:16**

"Now it is impossible to please God without faith, since anyone who comes to him must believe that he exists and rewards those who try to find him." **Hebrews 11:6**

"Pray constantly; and for all things give thanks to God, because this is what God expects you to do in Christ Jesus." **I Thessalonians 5:17-18**

"The prayer of faith will save the sick man and the Lord will raise him up again; and if he has committed any sins,

237

he will be forgiven. So confess your sins to one another, and pray for one another, and this will cure you; the heartfelt prayer of a good man works very powerfully."

James 5:15-16

"Ask, and it will be given to you; search, and you will find; knock, and the door will be opened to you. For the one who asks always receives; the one who searches always finds; the one who knocks will always have the door opened to him." **Matthew 7:7-8**

"And if you have faith, everything you ask for in prayer you will receive." **Matthew 21:22**

"I tell you solemnly once again, if two of you on earth agree to ask anything at all, it will be granted to you by my Father in heaven. For where two or three meet in my name, I shall be there with them." **Matthew 18:19-20**

"I tell you therefore: everything you ask and pray for, believe that you have it already, and it will be yours."

Mark 11:24

"If you remain in me and my words remain in you, you may ask what you will and you shall get it."

John 15:7

"I tell you most solemnly, anything you ask for from the Father he will grant in my name." **John 16:23b**

"Let us be confident, then, in approaching the throne of grace, that we shall have mercy from him and find grace when we are in need of help." **Hebrews 4:16**

"The salvation of the virtuous comes from Yahweh, he is their shelter when trouble comes; Yahweh helps and rescues them, he saves them because they take shelter in him." **Psalms 37[36]:39-40**

"I answer everyone who invokes me, I am with them when they are in trouble; I bring them safety and honor." **Psalms 91[90]:15**

"Standing close to all who invoke him, close to all who invoke Yahweh faithfully. Those who fear him need only to ask to be answered; he hears their cries for help and saves them." **Psalms 145[144]:18-19**

"Yahweh stands far from the wicked, but he listens to the prayers of the virtuous." **Proverbs 15:29**

"And whatever we ask him, we shall receive, because we keep his commandments and live the kind of life that he wants." **I John 3:22**

In Perseverance

"You will be hated by all men on account of my name, but not a hair of your head will be lost. Your endurance will win you your lives."   **Luke 21:17-19**

"You will be hated by all men on account of my name; but the man who stands firm to the end will be saved."
     Matthew 10:22

"Many false prophets will arise; they will deceive many, and with the increase of lawlessness, love in most men will grow cold."   **Matthew 24:11-12**

"All these joined in continuous prayer, together with several women, including Mary the mother of Jesus, and with his brothers."   **Acts 1:14**

"These remained faithful to the teaching of the apostles, to the brotherhood, to the breaking of bread and to the prayers."   **Acts 2:42**

"He will repay each one as his works deserve. For those who sought renown and honor and immortality by always doing good there will be eternal life; for the unsubmissive who refused to take truth for their guide and took depravity instead, there will be anger and fury."
     Romans 2:6-8

"Be persevering in your prayers and be thankful as you stay awake to pray."   **Colossians 4:2**

"Here is a saying that you can rely on: If we have died with him, then we shall live with him. If we hold firm, then we shall reign with him. If we disown him, then he will disown us." **II Timothy 2:11-12**

"But the man who looks steadily at the perfect law of freedom and makes that his habit – not listening and then forgetting, but actively putting it into practice – will be happy in all that he does." **James 1:25**

"Pray all the time, asking for what you need, praying in the Spirit on every possible occasion. Never get tired of staying awake to pray for all the saints."
Ephesians 6:18

"For you not only shared in the sufferings of those who were in prison, but you happily accepted being stripped of your belongings, knowing that you owned something that was better and lasting. Be as confident now, then, since the reward is so great. You will need endurance to do God's will and gain what he has promised."
Hebrews 10:34-36

"With so many witnesses in a great cloud on every side of us, we too, then, should throw off everything that hinders us, especially the sin that clings so easily, and keep running steadily in the race we have started. Let us not lose sight of Jesus, who leads us in our faith and brings it to perfection: for the sake of the joy which was still in the future, he endured the cross, disregarding the shamefulness of it, and from now on has taken his place at the right of God's throne. Think of the way he stood such opposition from sinners and then you will not give up for want of courage."
Hebrews 12:1-3

"I know all about you: how hard you work and how much you put up with. I know you cannot stand wicked men, and how you tested the impostors who called themselves apostles and proved they were liars. I know, too, that you have patience, and have suffered for my name without growing tired."   **Revelation 2:2-3**

"We have never failed to pray for you [...]. You will have in you the strength, based on his own glorious power, never to give in, but to bear anything joyfully, thanking the Father who has made it possible for you to join the saints and with them to inherit the light."   **Colossians 1:9b.11-12**

"Your faith is growing so wonderfully and the love that you have for one another never stops increasing; and among the churches of God we can take special pride in you for your constancy and faith under all the persecutions and troubles you have to bear. It all shows that God's judgement is just, and the purpose of it is that you may be found worthy of the kingdom of God; it is for the sake of this that you are suffering now."   **II Thessalonians 1:3b-5**

In Wisdom

"My son, if you take my words to heart, if you set store by my commandments, tuning your ear to wisdom, and applying your heart to truth: yes, if your plea is for clear perception, if you cry out for discernment, if you look for it as if it were silver, and search for it as for buried treasure, you will then understand what the fear of Yahweh is, and discover the knowledge of God. For Yahweh himself is giver of wisdom, from his mouth issue knowledge and discernment."   **Proverbs 2:1-6**

"When wisdom comes into your heart and knowledge is a delight to you, then prudence will be there to watch over you, and discernment be your guardian to keep you from the way that is evil, from the man whose speech is deceitful. [...] So you will pursue the way of good men, persisting in the paths of the virtuous. For the land will be for honest men to live in, the innocent will have it for their home."
Proverbs 2:10-12.20-21

"'The beginning of wisdom? The acquisition of wisdom; at the cost of all you have, acquire perception. Hold her close, and she will make you great; embrace her, and she will be your pride; she will set a crown of grace on your head, present you with a glorious diadem.'

Listen, my son, take my words to heart, and the years of your life shall be multiplied. I have educated you in the ways of wisdom, I have guided you along the paths of honesty."   **Proverbs 4:7-11**

"Look forward, therefore, to my words; yearn for them, and they will instruct you. Wisdom is bright, and does not

243

grow dim. By those who love her she is readily seen, and found by those who look for her. Quick to anticipate those who desire her, she makes herself known to them. [...] Even to think about her is understanding fully grown; be on the alert for her and anxiety will quickly leave you. [...] Of her the most sure beginning is the desire for discipline, care for discipline means loving her, loving her means keeping her laws, obeying her laws guarantees incorruptibility, incorruptibility brings near to God."

Wisdom 6:11-13.15.17-19

"For Wisdom is quicker to move than any motion; she is so pure, she pervades and permeates all things. She is a breath of the power of God, pure emanation of the glory of the Almighty; hence nothing impure can find a way into her. She is a reflection of the eternal light, untarnished mirror of God's active power, image of his goodness."

Wisdom 7:24-26

"In each generation she passes into holy souls, she makes them friends of God and prophets; for God loves only the man who lives with Wisdom." **Wisdom 7:27b-28**

"All wisdom is from the Lord, and it is his own for ever. [...] Shrewd understanding is everlasting."

Ecclesiasticus 1:1.5

"To fear the Lord is the beginning of wisdom, she was created with the faithful in their mothers' womb; she has made a nest among men, an age-old foundation, and to their offspring she will cling faithfully. To fear the Lord is the perfection of wisdom." **Ecclesiasticus 1:14-16a**

"He has showered down learning and discernment, and exalted the renown of those who hold her close To fear the Lord is the root of wisdom, and her branches are long life."
Ecclesiasticus 1:24-25

"If you desire wisdom, keep the commandments, and the Lord will convey her to you. For wisdom and instruction mean the fear of the Lord, and what pleases him is faithfulness and gentleness. Do not be unsubmissive to the fear of the Lord."
Ecclesiasticus 1:26-28a

"For wisdom and instruction mean the fear of the Lord, and what pleases him is faithfulness and gentleness."
Ecclesiasticus 1:33-35a

"My son, if you aspire to serve the Lord, prepare yourself for an ordeal. Be sincere of heart, be steadfast, and do not be alarmed when disaster comes." **Ecclesiasticus 2:1-2**

"Children, listen to me your father, do what I tell you, and so be safe."
Ecclesiasticus 3:1

"The heart of a sensible man will reflect on parables, an attentive ear is the sage's dream. Water quenches a blazing fire, almsgiving atones for sins." **Ecclesiasticus 3:31-32**

"And cares for those who seek her. Whoever loves her loves life, those who wait on her early will be filled with happiness. Whoever holds her close will inherit honor, and wherever he walks the Lord will bless him. Those who serve her minister to the Holy One, and the Lord loves those who love her. Whoever obeys her judges aright, and whoever pays attention to her dwells secure. If he trusts himself to her he will inherit her, and his descendants will remain in possession of her; for though she takes him at first through winding ways."   **Ecclesiasticus 4:12-17**

"My son, from your earliest youth choose instruction, and till your hair is white you will keep finding wisdom. Cultivate her like the plowman and the sower, and wait for her fine harvest, for in tilling her you will toil a little while, but very soon you will be eating her crops. [...] for discipline is true to her name, she is not accessible to many."

                    Ecclesiasticus 6:18-20.23

"If you give your mind to it, subtlety will be yours. If you love listening you will learn, if you lend an ear, wisdom will be yours. Attend the gathering of elders."

                    Ecclesiasticus 6:33-34

"Reflect on the injunctions of the Lord, busy yourself at all times with his commandments. He will strengthen your mind, and the wisdom you desire will be granted you."

                    Ecclesiasticus 6:37

"He pursues her like a hunter, and lies in wait by her path; he peeps in at her windows." **Ecclesiasticus 14:22-23**

"But before all this happens, men will seize you and persecute you; they will hand you over to the synagogues and to imprisonment, and bring you before kings and governors because of my name [...]. Keep this carefully in mind: you are not to prepare your defense, because I myself shall give you an eloquence and a wisdom that none of your opponents will be able to resist or contradict."

                    Luke 21:12.14-15

"The language of the cross may be illogical to those who are not on the way to salvation, but those of us who are on the way see it as God's power to save. As scripture says: I shall destroy the wisdom of the wise and bring to nothing all the learning of the learned. Where are the philosophers now? Where are the scribes? Where are any of our thinkers today? Do you see now how God has shown up the foolishness of human wisdom? If it was God's wisdom that human wisdom should not know God, it was because God wanted to save those who have faith through the foolishness of the message that we preach."   **I Corinthians 1:18-21**

"The human race has nothing to boast about to God, but God has made you members of Christ Jesus and by God's doing he has become our wisdom, and our virtue, and our holiness, and our freedom."   **I Corinthians 1:29-30**

"The hidden wisdom of God which we teach in our mysteries is the wisdom that God predestined to be for our glory before the ages began. It is a wisdom that none of the masters of this age have ever known, or they would not have crucified the Lord of Glory."   **I Corinthians 2:7-8**

"May the God of our Lord Jesus Christ, the Father of glory, give you a spirit of wisdom and perception of what is revealed, to bring you to full knowledge of him. May he enlighten the eyes of your mind so that you can see what hope his call holds for you, what rich glories he has promised the saints will inherit and how infinitely great is the power that he has exercised for us believers."
                    Ephesians 1:17-19a

"Let the message of Christ, in all its richness, find a home with you. Teach each other, and advise each other, in all wisdom. With gratitude in your hearts sing psalms and hymns and inspired songs to God." **Colossians 3:16**

"Be tactful with those who are not Christians and be sure you make the best use of your time with them. Talk to them agreeably and with a flavor of wit, and try to fit your answers to the needs of each one." **Colossians 4:5-6**

"If there is any one of you who needs wisdom, he must ask God, who gives to all freely and ungrudgingly; it will be given to him. But he must ask with faith, and no trace of doubt, because a person who has doubts is like the waves thrown up in the sea when the wind drives."
James 1:5-7

"Whereas the wisdom that comes down from above is essentially something pure; it also makes for peace, and is kindly and considerate; it is full of compassion and shows itself by doing good; nor is there any trace of partiality or hypocrisy in it." **James 3:17**

In Strength

"God is our shelter, our strength, ever ready to help in time of trouble, so we shall not be afraid when the earth gives way, when mountains tumble into the depths of the sea, and its waters roar and seethe, the mountains tottering as it heaves. (Yahweh Sabaoth is on our side, our citadel, the God of Jacob!)." **Psalms 46[45]:1-3**

"I need only say, 'I am slipping,' and your love, Yahweh, immediately supports me." **Psalms 94[93]:18**

"Blessed be Yahweh, my rock, who trains my hands for war [...], my love, my bastion, my citadel, my savior." **Psalms 144[143]:1a.2a**

"Yahweh my Lord is my strength, he makes my feet as light as a doe's, he sets my steps on the heights." **Habakkuk 3:19**

"Yahweh is a stronghold for the man of honest life." **Proverbs 10:29a**

"Yahweh roars from Zion, makes his voice heard from Jerusalem; heaven and earth tremble. But Yahweh will be a shelter for his people, a stronghold for the sons of Israel." **Joel 4:16**

"Do not be afraid, for I have redeemed you; I have called you by your name, you are mine. [...] For I am Yahweh, your God, [...]. Because you are precious in my eyes, because you are honored and I love you, I give men in exchange for you, peoples in return for your life." **Isaiah 43:1b.3a.4**

"Trust in Yahweh for ever, for Yahweh is the everlasting Rock." **Isaiah 26:4**

"These are the trials through which we triumph, by the power of him who loved us. For I am certain of this: neither death nor life, no angel, no prince, nothing that exists, nothing still to come, not any power, or height or depth, nor any created thing, can ever come between us and the love of God made visible in Christ Jesus our Lord."
Romans 8:37-39

"Because the face of the Lord frowns on evil men, but the eyes of the Lord are turned toward the virtuous, his ears to their cry." **I Peter 3:12**

In Fidelity

"My son, do not forget my teaching, let your heart keep my principles, for these will give you lengthier days, longer years of life, and greater happiness. Let kindliness and loyalty never leave you: tie them around your neck, write them on the tablet of your heart."　**Proverbs 3:1-3**

"What sort of servant, then, is faithful and wise enough for the master to place him over his household to give them their food at the proper time?"　**Matthew 24:45**

"His master said to him, 'Well done, good and faithful servant; you have shown you can be faithful in small things, I will trust you with greater; come and join in your master's happiness."　**Matthew 25:21**

"The man who can be trusted in little things can be trusted in great; the man who is dishonest in little things will be dishonest in great."　**Luke 16:10**

"'Well done, my good servant!' he replied. 'Since you have proved yourself faithful in a very small thing, you shall have the government of ten cities.'"
Luke 19:17

"People must think of us as Christ's servants, stewards entrusted with the mysteries of God. What is expected of stewards is that each one should be found worthy of his trust."
I Corinthians 4:1-2

"Even if you have to die, keep faithful, and I will give you the crown of life for your prize."

Revelation 2:10d

"And they will go to war against the Lamb; but the Lamb is the Lord of lords and the King of kings, and he will defeat them and they will be defeated by his followers, the called, the chosen, the faithful."   **Revelation 17:14**

"What the Spirit brings is very different: love, joy, peace, patience, kindness, goodness, trustfulness, gentleness and self-control. There can be no law against things like that, of course. You cannot belong to Christ Jesus unless you crucify all self-indulgent passions and desires. Since the Spirit is our life, let us be directed by the Spirit."

Galatians 5:22-25

Part III

Part II

1

Plan of Salvation

God is Holy

"Speak to the whole community of the sons of Israel and say to them: 'Be holy, for I, Yahweh your God, am holy.'"
Leviticus 19:2

"You shall treat him as holy, for he offers up the food of your God. He shall be a holy person to you, because I, Yahweh, am holy, who sanctify you." **Leviticus 21:8**

"There is none as holy as Yahweh."
I Samuel 2:2a

"And they cried out one to another in this way, 'Holy, holy, holy is Yahweh Sabaoth. His glory fills the whole earth.'"
Isaiah 6:3

"Cry out for joy and gladness, you dwellers in Zion, for great in the midst of you is the Holy One of Israel."
Isaiah 12:6

"For I am God, not man: I am the Holy One in your midst and have no wish to destroy."
Hosea 11:9b

"Be holy in all you do, since it is the Holy One who has called you, and scripture says: Be holy, for I am holy."
I Peter 1:15-16

"Each of the four animals had six wings and had eyes all the way around as well as inside; and day and night they never stopped singing: 'Holy, Holy, Holy is the Lord God, the Almighty; he was, he is and he is to come.'"
Revelation 4:8

"Who would not revere and praise your name, O Lord? You alone are holy, and all the pagans will come and adore you for the many acts of justice you have shown."
Revelation 15:4

God Created Man
in His Image and Likeness

"God said, 'Let us make man in our own image, in the likeness of ourselves, and let them be masters of the fish of the sea, the birds of heaven, the cattle, all the wild beasts and all the reptiles that crawl upon the earth.' God created man in the image of himself, in the image of God he created him, male and female he created them. God blessed them, saying to them, 'Be fruitful, multiply, fill the earth and conquer it.'"   **Genesis 1:26-28a**

"Yet God did make man imperishable, he made him in the image of his own nature."   **Wisdom 2:23**

"And we, with our unveiled faces reflecting like mirrors the brightness of the Lord, all grow brighter and brighter as we are turned into the image that we reflect; this is the work of the Lord who is Spirit."   **II Corinthians 3:18**

"And we, who have been modeled on the earthly man, will be modeled on the heavenly man."
I Corinthians 15:49

"They are the ones he chose specially long ago and intended to become true images of his Son, so that his Son might be the eldest of many brothers."
Romans 8:29

Precept of God: Obedience

"Yahweh God took the man and settled him in the garden of Eden to cultivate and take care of it. Then Yahweh God gave the man this admonition, 'You may eat indeed of all the trees in the garden. Nevertheless of the tree of the Knowledge of good and evil you are not to eat, for on the day you eat of it you shall most surely die.'"

Genesis 2:15-17

Man's Answer to God: Disobedience

"The serpent was the most subtle of all the wild beasts that Yahweh God had made. It asked the woman, 'Did God really say you were not to eat from any of the trees in the garden?' The woman answered the serpent, 'We may eat the fruit of the trees in the garden. But of the fruit of the tree in the middle of the garden God said, 'You must not eat it, nor touch it, under pain of death.' Then the serpent said to the woman, 'No! You will not die! God knows in fact that on the day you eat it your eyes will be opened and you will be like gods, knowing good and evil.' The woman saw that the tree was good to eat and pleasing to the eye, and that it was desirable for the knowledge that it could give. So she took some of its fruit and ate it. She gave some also to her husband who was with her, and he ate it."

Genesis 3:1-6

Consequence of Sin: Death

"To the woman he said: 'I will multiply your pains in childbearing, you shall give birth to your children in pain. Your yearning shall be for your husband, yet he will lord it over you.' To the man he said, 'Because you listened to the voice of your wife and ate from the tree of which I had forbidden you to eat, accursed be the soil because of you. With suffering shall you get your food from it every day of your life. It shall yield you brambles and thistles, and you shall eat wild plants. With sweat on your brow shall you eat your bread, until you return to the soil, as you were taken from it. For dust you are and to dust you shall return.' [...] So Yahweh God expelled him from the garden of Eden, to till the soil from which he had been taken. He banished the man, and in front of the garden of Eden he posted the cherubs, and the flame of a flashing sword, to guard the way to the tree of life."   **Genesis 3:16-19.23-24**

"For the wage paid by sin is death."
                                        Romans 6:23a

"It was the devil's envy that brought death into the world, as those who are his partners will discover."
                                        Wisdom 2:24

Sin: the Heritage That Contaminated Mankind – We Are All Sinners

"Well then, sin entered the world through one man, and through sin death, and thus death has spread through the whole human race because everyone has sinned."
Romans 5:12

"Well: are we any better off? Not at all: as we said before, Jews and Greeks are all under sin's dominion. As scripture says: There is not a good man left, no, not one: there is not one who understands, not one who looks for God. All have turned aside, tainted all alike; there is not one good man left, not a single one." **Romans 3:9-12**

"Both Jew and pagan sinned and forfeited God's glory."
Romans 3:23

"If it is certain that death reigned over everyone as the consequence of one man's fall." **Romans 5:17a**

"Again, as one man's fall brought condemnation on everyone." **Romans 5:18a**

The Price of Our Salvation: the Blood of Jesus

"In fact, according to the Law almost everything has to be purified with blood; and if there is no shedding of blood, there is no remission." **Hebrews 9:22**

"And yet ours were the sufferings he bore, ours the sorrows he carried. But we, we thought of him as someone punished, struck by God, and brought low. Yet he was pierced through for our faults, crushed for our sins. On him lies a punishment that brings us peace, and through his wounds we are healed. We had all gone astray like sheep, each taking his own way, and Yahweh burdened him with the sins of all of us." **Isaiah 53:4-6**

"Since it is the same justice of God that comes through faith to everyone, Jew and pagan alike, who believes in Jesus Christ. Both Jew and pagan sinned and forfeited God's glory, and both are justified through the free gift of his grace by being redeemed in Christ Jesus who was appointed by God to sacrifice his life so as to win reconciliation through faith. In this way God makes his justice known; first, for the past, when sins went unpunished because he held his hand." **Romans 3:22-25**

"For our sake God made the sinless one into sin, so that in him we might become the goodness of God." **II Corinthians 5:21**

"Christ redeemed us from the curse of the Law by being cursed for our sake, since scripture says: 'Cursed be everyone who is hanged on a tree.'" **Galatians 3:13**

"Then he took a cup, and when he had returned thanks he gave it to them. 'Drink all of you from this,' he said, 'for this is my blood, the blood of the covenant, which is to be poured out for many for the forgiveness of sins."

Matthew 26:27-28

"In whom, through his blood, we gain our freedom, the forgiveness of our sins. Such is the richness of the grace."

Ephesians 1:7

"But now Christ has come, as the high priest of all the blessings which were to come. He has passed through the greater, the more perfect tent, which is better than the one made by men's hands because it is not of this created order; and he has entered the sanctuary once and for all, taking with him not the blood of goats and bull calves, but his own blood, having won an eternal redemption for us."

Hebrews 9:11-12

"In other words, brothers, through the blood of Jesus we have the right to enter the sanctuary, by a new way which he has opened for us, a living opening through the curtain, that is to say, his body." **Hebrews 10:19-20**

"Remember, the ransom that was paid to free you from the useless way of life your ancestors handed down was not paid in anything corruptible, neither in silver nor gold, but in the precious blood of a lamb without spot or stain, namely Christ." **I Peter1:18-19**

"The blood of Jesus, his Son, purifies us from all sin."

I John 1:7b

"If we say we have no sin in us, we are deceiving ourselves and refusing to admit the truth; but if we acknowledge our sins, then God who is faithful and just will forgive our sins and purify us from everything that is wrong."

I John 1:8-9

"From Jesus Christ, the faithful witness, the First-born from the dead, the Ruler of the kings of the earth."

Revelation 1:5a

"They sang a new hymn: 'You are worthy to take the scroll and break the seals of it, because you were sacrificed, and with your blood you bought men for God of every race, language, people and nation.'" **Revelation 5:9**

Conversion: the Way to Salvation

"Go and learn the meaning of the words: What I want is mercy, not sacrifice. And indeed I did not come to call the virtuous, but sinners." **Matthew 9:13**

"After John and been arrested, Jesus went into Galilee. There he proclaimed the Good News from God. 'The time has come,' he said, 'and the kingdom of God is close at hand. Repent, and believe the Good News.'" **Mark 1:14-15**

"He went through the whole Jordan district proclaiming a baptism of repentance for the forgiveness of sins." **Luke 3:3**

"Urging both Jews and Greeks to turn to God and to believe in our Lord Jesus." **Acts 20:21**

"On the contrary I started preaching first to the people of Damascus, then to those of Jerusalem and all the countryside of Judaea, and also to the pagans, urging them to repent and turn to God, proving their change of heart by their deeds." **Acts 26:20**

"Do you think you will escape God's judgment? Or are you abusing his abundant goodness, patience and toleration, not realizing that this goodness of God is meant to lead you to repentance?" **Romans 2:3b-4**

"The Lord is not being slow to carry out his promises, as anybody else might be called slow; but he is being patient with you all, wanting nobody to be lost and everybody to be brought to change his ways."   **II Peter 3:9**

"'You must repent,' Peter answered, 'and every one of you must be baptized in the name of Jesus Christ for the forgiveness of your sins, and you will receive the gift of the Holy Spirit.'"   **Acts 2:38**

"Now you must repent and turn to God, so that your sins may be wiped out."   **Acts 3:19**

"I shall deliver you from the people and from the pagans, to whom I am sending you to open their eyes, so that they may turn from darkness to light, from the dominion of Satan to God, and receive, through faith in me, forgiveness of their sins and a share in the inheritance of the sanctified."
      Acts 26:17-18

"In the same way, I tell you, there will be more rejoicing in heaven over one repentant sinner than over ninety-nine virtuous men who have no need of repentance."
      Luke 15:7

"In the same way, I tell you, there is rejoicing among the angels of God over one repentant sinner."
      Luke 15:10

"The nearer you go to God, the nearer he will come to you. Clean your hands, you sinners, and clear your minds, you waverers. Look at your wretched condition, and weep for it in misery; be miserable instead of laughing, gloomy instead of happy. Humble yourselves before the Lord and he will lift you up."   **James 4:8-10**

The Love of God for Us

"Yes, God loved the world so much that he gave his only Son, so that everyone who believes in him may not be lost but may have eternal life."　**John 3:16**

"God's love for us was revealed when God sent into the world his only Son so that we could have life through him; this is the love I mean: not our love for God, but God's love for us when he sent his Son to be the sacrifice that takes our sins away."　**I John 4:9-10**

"And this hope is not deceptive, because the love of God has been poured into our hearts by the Holy Spirit which has been given us."　**Romans 5:5**

"But what proves that God loves us is that Christ died for us while we were still sinners."　**Romans 5:8**

"But God loved us with so much love that he was generous with his mercy: when we were dead through our sins, he brought us to life with Christ – it is through grace that you have been saved."　**Ephesians 2:4-5**

"For I am certain of this: neither death nor life, no angel, no prince, nothing that exists, nothing still to come, not any power, or height or depth, nor any created thing, can ever come between us and the love of God made visible in Christ Jesus our Lord."　**Romans 8:38-39**

Jesus Died for Us, Sinners

"And indeed I did not come to call the virtuous, but sinners."   **Matthew 9:13c**

"When Jesus heard this he said to them, 'It is not the healthy who need the doctor, but the sick. I did not come to call the virtuous, but sinners.'"   **Mark 2:17**

"Jesus said to them in reply, 'It is not those who are well who need the doctor, but the sick. I have not come to call the virtuous, but sinners to repentance.'"   **Luke 5:31-32**

"Here is a saying that you can rely on and nobody should doubt: that Christ Jesus came into the world to save sinners. I myself am the greatest of them."   **I Timothy 1:15**

"Well then, in the first place, I taught you what I had been taught myself, namely that Christ died for our sins, in accordance with the scriptures; that he was buried; and that he was raised to life on the third day, in accordance with the scriptures."   **I Corinthians 15:3-4**

"For God sent his Son into the world not to condemn the world, but so that through him the world might be saved."   **John 3:17**

"It is to him that all the prophets bear this witness: that all who believe in Jesus will have their sins forgiven through his name."   **Acts 10:43**

"I am writing this, my children, to stop you sinning; but if anyone should sin, we have our advocate with the Father, Jesus Christ, who is just; he is the sacrifice that takes our sins away, and not only ours, but the whole world's."

I John 2:1-2

The Blood of Jesus Reconciles Us with God and We Become Upright in His Eyes

"So far then we have seen that, through our Lord Jesus Christ, by faith we are judged righteous and at peace with God."
Romans 5:1

"Having died to make us righteous, is it likely that he would now fail to save us from God's anger? When we were reconciled to God by the death of his Son, we were still enemies; now that we have been reconciled, surely we may count on being saved by the life of his Son? Not merely because we have been reconciled but because we are filled with joyful trust in God, through our Lord Jesus Christ, through whom we have already gained our reconciliation."
Romans 5:9-11

"It is all God's work. It was God who reconciled us to himself through Christ. [...] In other words, God in Christ was reconciling the world to himself, not holding men's faults against them."
II Corinthians 5:18a.19a

"God were appealing through us, and the appeal that we make in Christ's name is: be reconciled to God. For our sake God made the sinless one into sin, so that in him we might become the goodness of God."
II Corinthians 5:20b-21

"Because that is what he has done: he has taken us out of the power of darkness and created a place for us in the kingdom of the Son that he loves, and in him, we gain our freedom, the forgiveness of our sins."

Colossians 1:13-14

"Because God wanted all perfection to be found in him and all things to be reconciled through him and for him, everything in heaven and everything on earth, when he made peace by his death on the cross." **Colossians 1:19-20**

"But God has made you members of Christ Jesus and by God's doing he has become our wisdom, and our virtue, and our holiness, and our freedom."

I Corinthians 1:30

"You know perfectly well that people who do wrong will not inherit the kingdom of God. [...] These are the sort of people some of you were once, but now you have been washed clean, and sanctified, and justified through the name of the Lord Jesus Christ and through the Spirit of our God." **I Corinthians 6:9a.11**

We Receive Salvation through Faith in Jesus Christ

"But to all who did accept him he gave power to become children of God, to all who believe in the name of him."
John 1:12

"He who believes and is baptized will be saved; he who does not believe will be condemned."
Mark 16:16

"I have told you already: You will die in your sins. Yes, if you do not believe that I am He, you will die in your sins."
John 8:24

"It is to him that all the prophets bear this witness: that all who believe in Jesus will have their sins forgiven through his name."   **Acts 10:43**

"My brothers, I want you to realize that it is through him that forgiveness of your sins is proclaimed. Through him justification from all sins which the Law of Moses was unable to justify is offered to every believer."
Acts 13:38-39

"They told him, 'Become a believer in the Lord Jesus, and you will be saved, and your household too.'"
Acts 16:31

"I have written all this to you so that you who believe in the name of the Son of God may be sure that you have eternal life." **I John 5:13**

"When Jesus reached the spot he looked up and spoke to him: 'Zacchaeus, come down. Hurry, because I must stay at your house today.' And he hurried down and welcomed him joyfully. [...] And Jesus said to him, 'Today salvation has come to this house, because this man too is a son of Abraham; for the Son of Man has come to seek out and save what was lost.'" **Luke 19:5-6.9-10**

"Anyone who believes in the Son has eternal life, but anyone who refuses to believe in the Son will never see life: the anger of God stays on him." **John 3:36**

"Yes, God loved the world so much that he gave his only Son, so that everyone who believes in him may not be lost but may have eternal life." **John 3:16**

"For God sent his Son into the world not to condemn the world, but so that through him the world might be saved." **John 3:17**

"No one who believes in him will be condemned; but whoever refuses to believe is condemned already, because he has refused to believe in the name of God's only Son." **John 3:18**

"Because it is by grace that you have been saved, through faith; not by anything of your own, but by a gift from God; not by anything that you have done, so that nobody can claim the credit." **Ephesians 2:8-9**

"This is the testimony: God has given us eternal life and this life is in his Son; anyone who has the Son has life, anyone who does not have the Son does not have life."

I John 5:11-12

"Look, I am standing at the door, knocking. If one of you hears me calling and opens the door, I will come in to share his meal, side by side with him."

Revelation 3:20

Witness: Confession and Proclamation of Jesus Christ as Savior and Lord

"On the positive side it says: The word, that is the faith we proclaim, is very near to you, it is on your lips and in your heart. If your lips confess that Jesus is Lord and if you believe in your heart that God raised him from the dead, then you will be saved. By believing from the heart you are made righteous; by confessing with your lips you are saved."

Romans 10:8-10

"God raised this man Jesus to life, and all of us are witnesses to that. Now raised to the heights by God's right hand, he has received from the Father the Holy Spirit, who was promised, and what you see and hear is the outpouring of that Spirit. [...] For this reason the whole House of Israel can be certain that God has made this Jesus whom you crucified both Lord and Christ." **Acts 2:32-33.36**

"This is the stone rejected by you the builders, but which has proved to be the keystone. For of all the names in the world given to men, this is the only one by which we can be saved." **Acts 4:11-12**

"When scripture says: those who believe in him will have no cause for shame, it makes no distinction between Jew and Greek: all belong to the same Lord who is rich enough, however many ask his help, for everyone who calls on the name of the Lord will be saved." **Romans 10:11-13**

"For if anyone in this adulterous and sinful generation is ashamed of me and of my words, the Son of Man will also be ashamed of him when he comes in the glory of his Father with the holy angels."   **Mark 8:38**

"So if anyone declares himself for me in the presence of men, I will declare myself for him in the presence of my Father in heaven. But the one who disowns me in the presence of men, I will disown in the presence of my Father in heaven."   **Matthew 10:32-33**

"Because no one who has the Father can deny the Son, and to acknowledge the Son is to have the Father as well."

I John 2:23

The Supremacy of Jesus: Obedience to His Word

"If you love me you will keep my commandments."
John 14:15

"Anybody who receives my commandments and keeps them will be one who loves me; and anybody who loves me will be loved by my Father, and I shall love him and show myself to him. [...] 'If anyone loves me he will keep my word, and my Father will love him, and we shall come to him and make our home with him. Those who do not love me do not keep my words. And my word is not my own: it is the word of the one who sent me.'" **John 14:21.23b-24**

"It is not those who say to me, 'Lord, Lord,' who will enter the kingdom of heaven, but the person who does the will of my Father in heaven." **Matthew 7:21**

"Therefore, everyone who listens to these words of mine and acts on them will be like a sensible man who built his house on rock." **Matthew 7:24**

"Everyone who comes to me and listens to my words and acts on them – I will show you what he is like. He is like the man who when he built his house dug, and dug deep, and laid the foundations on rock; when the river was in flood it bore down on that house but could not shake it, it was so well built." **Luke 6:47-48**

"Why do you call me, 'Lord, Lord' and not do what I say?" **Luke 6:46**

"A child of God listens to the words of God; if you refuse to listen, it is because you are not God's children."
John 8:47

"But he said in answer, 'My mother and my brothers are those who hear the word of God and put it into practice.'"
Luke 8:21

"So do away with all the impurities and bad habits that are still left in you – accept and submit to the word which has been planted in you and can save your souls. But you must do what the word tells you, and not just listen to it and deceive yourselves."   **James 1:21-22**

"To listen to the word and not obey is like looking at your own features in a mirror and then, after a quick look, going off and immediately forgetting what you looked like. But the man who looks steadily at the perfect law of freedom and makes that his habit – not listening and then forgetting, but actively putting it into practice – will be happy in all that he does."   **James 1:23-25**

"I know all about you; and now I have opened in front of you a door that nobody will be able to close – and I know that though you are not very strong, you have kept my commandments and not disowned my name."
Revelation 3:8

Jesus Christ Gives Us Eternal Life

"And what is promised to you by his own promise is eternal life." **I John 2:25**

"This is the testimony: God has given us eternal life and this life is in his Son; anyone who has the Son has life, anyone who does not have the Son does not have life. I have written all this to you so that you who believe in the name of the Son of God may be sure that you have eternal life." **I John 5:11-13**

"Jesus said: 'I am the resurrection. If anyone believes in me, even though he dies he will live, and whoever lives and believes in me will never die. Do you believe this?'" **John 11:25-26**

"Yes, it is my Father's will that whoever sees the Son and believes in him shall have eternal life, and that I shall raise him up on the last day." **John 6:40**

"I am the living bread which has come down from heaven. Anyone who eats this bread will live for ever; and the bread that I shall give is my flesh, for the life of the world." **John 6:51**

"I tell you most solemnly, whoever keeps my word will never see death." **John 8:51**

"I tell you most solemnly, the hour will come – in fact it is here already – when the dead will hear the voice of the Son of God, and all who hear it will live."
John 5:25

"Do not work for food that cannot last, but work for food that endures to eternal life, the kind of food the Son of Man is offering you, for on him the Father, God himself, has set his seal." **John 6:27**

"I tell you most solemnly, everybody who believes has eternal life." **John 6:47**

"Now, however, you have been set free from sin, you have been made slaves of God, and you get a reward leading to your sanctification and ending in eternal life. For the wage paid by sin is death; the present given by God is eternal life in Christ Jesus our Lord." **Romans 6:22-23**

"The sheep that belong to me listen to my voice; I know them and they follow me. I give them eternal life; they will never be lost and no one will ever steal them from me."
John 10:27-28

"I am the living bread which has come down from heaven. Anyone who eats this bread will live for ever; and the bread that I shall give is my flesh, for the life of the world. Then the Jews started arguing with one another: 'How can this man give us his flesh to eat?' they said. Jesus replied: 'I tell you most solemnly, if you do not eat the flesh of the Son of Man and drink his blood, you will not have life in you. Anyone who does eat my flesh and drink my blood has eternal life, and I shall raise him up on the last day.'"
John 6:51-54

"Yes, God loved the world so much that he gave his only Son, so that everyone who believes in him may not be lost but may have eternal life." **John 3:16**

"Anyone who drinks the water that I shall give will never be thirsty again: the water that I shall give will turn into a spring inside him, welling up to eternal life." **John 4:14**

"I tell you most solemnly, whoever listens to my words, and believes in the one who sent me, has eternal life; without being brought to judgement he has passed from death to life." **John 5:24**

"It was for no reason except his own compassion that he saved us, by means of the cleansing water of rebirth and by renewing us with the Holy Spirit [...]. He did this so that we should be justified by his grace, to become heirs looking forward to inheriting eternal life." **Titus 3:5b.7**

"We know, too, that the Son of God has come, and has given us the power to know the true God. We are in the true God, as we are in his Son, Jesus Christ. This is the true God, this is eternal life." **I John 5:20**

Jesus Christ Promises and Sends the Holy Spirit

"I baptize you in water for repentance, but the one who follows me is more powerful than I am, and I am not fit to carry his sandals; he will baptize you with the Holy Spirit and fire."   **Matthew 3:11**

"In the course of his preaching he said, 'Someone is following me, someone who is more powerful than I am, and I am not fit to kneel down and undo the strap of his sandals. I have baptized you with water, but he will baptize you with the Holy Spirit.'"   **Mark 1:7-8**

"John also declared, 'I saw the Spirit coming down on him from heaven like a dove and resting on him. I did not know him myself, but he who sent me to baptize with water had said to me, 'The man on whom you see the Spirit come down and rest is the one who is going to baptize with the Holy Spirit.' Yes, I have seen and I am the witness that he is the Chosen One of God."   **John 1:32-34**

"Since he whom God has sent speaks God's own words: God gives him the Spirit without reserve."
John 3:34

"Still, I must tell you the truth: it is for your own good that I am going because unless I go, the Advocate will not come to you; but if I do go, I will send him to you."
John 16:7

"I shall ask the Father, and he will give you another Advocate to be with you for ever, that Spirit of truth whom

the world can never receive since it neither sees nor knows him; but you know him, because he is with you, he is in you."
John 14:16-17

"The Advocate, the Holy Spirit, whom the Father will send in my name, will teach you everything and remind you of all I have said to you."   **John 14:26**

"When the Advocate comes, whom I shall send to you from the Father, the Spirit of truth who issues from the Father, he will be my witness."   **John 15:26**

"But when the Spirit of truth comes he will lead you to the complete truth, since he will not be speaking as from himself but will say only what he has learned; and he will tell you of the things to come."
John 16:13

"John baptized with water but you, not many days from now, will be baptized with the Holy Spirit."
Acts 1:5

"But you will receive power when the Holy Spirit comes on you, and then you will be my witnesses not only in Jerusalem but throughout Judaea and Samaria, and indeed to the ends of the earth."   **Acts 1:8**

"When Pentecost day came around, they had all met in one room, when suddenly they heard what sounded like a powerful wind from heaven, the noise of which filled the entire house in which they were sitting; and something appeared to them that seemed like tongues of fire; these

separated and came to rest on the head of each of them. They were all filled with the Holy Spirit, and began to speak foreign languages as the Spirit gave them the gift of speech."
Acts 2:1-4

"We are witnesses to all this, we and the Holy Spirit whom God has given to those who obey him."
Acts 5:32

"When the apostles in Jerusalem heard that Samaria had accepted the word of God, they sent Peter and John to them, and they went down there, and prayed for the Samaritans to receive the Holy Spirit, for as yet he had not come down on any of them: they had only been baptized in the name of the Lord Jesus. Then they laid hands on them, and they received the Holy Spirit." **Acts 8:14-17**

"While Peter was still speaking the Holy Spirit came down on all the listeners. Jewish believers who had accompanied Peter were all astonished that the gift of the Holy Spirit should be poured out on the pagans too, since they could hear them speaking strange languages and proclaiming the greatness of God. Peter himself then said, 'Could anyone refuse the water of baptism to these people, now they have received the Holy Spirit just as much as we have?'" **Acts 10:44-47**

"I had scarcely begun to speak when the Holy Spirit came down on them in the same way as it came on us at the beginning, and I remembered that the Lord had said, 'John baptized with water, but you will be baptized with the Holy Spirit.'" **Acts 11:15-16**

The Promise of the Holy Spirit Is Also for Us

"I shall give you a new heart, and put a new spirit in you; I shall remove the heart of stone from your bodies and give you a heart of flesh instead. I shall put my spirit in you, and make you keep my laws and sincerely respect my observances."
Ezekiel 36:26-27

"But you will receive power when the Holy Spirit comes on you, and then you will be my witnesses not only in Jerusalem but throughout Judaea and Samaria, and indeed to the ends of the earth."
Acts 1:8

"'You must repent,' Peter answered, 'and every one of you must be baptized in the name of Jesus Christ for the forgiveness of your sins, and you will receive the gift of the Holy Spirit.' The promise that was made is for you and your children, and for all those who are far away, for all those whom the Lord our God will call to himself.'"
Acts 2:38-39

"We are witnesses to all this, we and the Holy Spirit whom God has given to those who obey him."
Acts 5:32

"So I say to you: Ask, and it will be given to you; search, and you will find; knock, and the door will be opened to you. For the one who asks always receives; the one who searches always finds; the one who knocks will always have the door opened to him. What father among you would hand his son a stone when he asked for bread? Or hand him a snake instead of a fish? Or hand him a scorpion if he asked for an egg? If you then, who are evil, know how to give your children what is good, how much more will the heavenly Father give the Holy Spirit to those who ask him!"

Luke 11:9-13

"I tell you therefore: everything you ask and pray for, believe that you have it already, and it will be yours."

Mark 11:24

"This was done so that in Christ Jesus the blessing of Abraham might include the pagans, and so that through faith we might receive the promised Spirit."

Galatians 3:14

"Now you too, in him, have heard the message of the truth and the good news of your salvation, and have believed it; and you too have been stamped with the seal of the Holy Spirit of the Promise, the pledge of our inheritance which brings freedom for those whom God has taken for his own, to make his glory praised."   **Ephesians 1:13-14**

"Marking us with his seal and giving us the pledge, the Spirit, that we carry in our hearts."   **II Corinthians 1:22**

"And this hope is not deceptive, because the love of God has been poured into our hearts by the Holy Spirit which has been given us."   **Romans 5:5**

"Do not drug yourselves with wine; this is simply dissipation; be filled with the Spirit."

Ephesians 5:18

"Didn't you realize that you were God's temple and that the Spirit of God was living among you?"

I Corinthians 3:16

"Your body, you know, is the temple of the Holy Spirit, who is in you since you received him from God. You are not your own property." **I Corinthians 6:19**

"Go, therefore, make disciples of all the nations; baptize them in the name of the Father and of the Son and of the Holy Spirit, and teach them to observe all the commandments I gave you. And know that I am with you always; yes, to the end of time." **Matthew 28:19-20**

We Are Children of God

"But to all who did accept him he gave power to become children of God, to all who believe in the name of him."
John 1:12

"So then, my brothers, there is no necessity for us to obey our unspiritual selves or to live unspiritual lives. If you do live in that way, you are doomed to die; but if by the Spirit you put an end to the misdeeds of the body you will live. Everyone moved by the Spirit is a son of God. The spirit you received is not the spirit of slaves bringing fear into your lives again; it is the spirit of sons, and it makes us cry out, 'Abba, Father!' The Spirit himself and our spirit bear united witness that we are children of God. And if we are children we are heirs as well: heirs of God and coheirs with Christ, sharing his sufferings so as to share his glory."
Romans 8:12-17

"And you are, all of you, sons of God through faith in Christ Jesus."
Galatians 3:26

"The proof that you are sons is that God has sent the Spirit of his Son into our hearts: the Spirit that cries, 'Abba, Father,' and it is this that makes you a son, you are not a slave any more; and if God has made you son, then he has made you heir."
Galatians 4:6-7

"Determining that we should become his adopted sons, through Jesus Christ for his own kind purposes."
Ephesians 1:5

"Think of the love that the Father has lavished on us, by letting us be called God's children; and that is what we

are. Because the world refused to acknowledge him, therefore it does not acknowledge us. My dear people, we are already the children of God but what we are to be in the future has not yet been revealed; all we know is, that when it is revealed we shall be like him because we shall see him as he really is."
                                        I John 3:1-2

"They are the ones he chose specially long ago and intended to become true images of his Son, so that his Son might be the eldest of many brothers."
                                        Romans 8:29

"Anyone who does the will of my Father in heaven, he is my brother and sister and mother."
                                        Matthew 12:50

"Jesus said to her, 'Do not cling to me, because I have not yet ascended to the Father. But go and find the brothers, and thell them: I am ascending to my Father and your Father, to my God and your God.'"
                                        John 20:17

"For the Lord trains the ones that he loves and he punishes all those that he acknowledge as his sons. Suffering is part of your training; God is treating you as his sons. Has there ever been any son whose father did not train him?"
                                        Hebrews 12:6-7

"Besides, we have all had our human fathers who punished us, and we respected them for it; we ought to be even more willing to submit ourselves to our spiritual Father, to be given life."
                                        Hebrews 12:9

God Wants Us Holy

"You must make yourselves holy, for I am Yahweh your God. You must keep my laws and put them into practice, for it is I, Yahweh, who make you holy."
Leviticus 20:7-8

"You must therefore be perfect just as your heavenly Father is perfect." **Matthew 5:48**

"To you all, then, who are God's beloved in Rome, called to be saints, may God our Father and the Lord Jesus Christ send grace and peace." **Romans 1:7**

"Think of God's mercy, my brothers, and worship him, I beg you, in a way that is worthy of thinking beings, by offering your living bodies as a holy sacrifice, truly pleasing to God." **Romans 12:1**

"To the church of God in Corinth, to the holy people of Jesus Christ, who are called to take their place among all the saints everywhere who pray to our Lord Jesus Christ; for he is their Lord no less than ours. May God our Father and the Lord Jesus Christ send you grace and peace"
I Corinthians 1:2-3

"Blessed be God the Father of our Lord Jesus Christ, who has blessed us with all the spiritual blessings of heaven in Christ. Before the world was made, he chose us, chose us in Christ, to be holy and spotless, and to live through love in his presence." **Ephesians 1:3-4**

"So you are no longer aliens or foreign visitors: you are citizens like all the saints, and part of God's household."

Ephesians 2:19

"Thanking the Father who has made it possible for you to join the saints and with them to inherit the light."

Colossians 1:12

"Not long ago, you were foreigners and enemies, in the way that you used to think and the evil things that you did; but now he has reconciled you, by his death and in that mortal body. Now you are able to appear before him holy, pure and blameless."   **Colossians 1:21-22**

"Who has saved us and called us to be holy – not because of anything we ourselves have done but for his own purpose and by his own grace. This grace had already been granted to us, in Christ Jesus, before the beginning of time."

II Timothy 1:9

"That is why all you who are holy brothers and have had the same heavenly call should turn your minds to Jesus, the apostle and the high priest of our religion."

Hebrews 3:1

"Be holy in all you do, since it is the Holy One who has called you, and scripture says: Be holy, for I am holy."

I Peter 1:15-16

"But you are a chosen race, a royal priesthood, a consecrated nation, a people set apart to sing the praises of

God who called you out of the darkness into his wonderful light."   **I Peter 2:9**

"Since everything is coming to an end like this, you should be living holy and saintly lives while you wait and long for the Day of God to come, when the sky will dissolve in flames and the elements melt in the heat."
                                      II Peter 3:11-12

2

Prayers

Asking to Receive Jesus Christ as Our Only Savior and Lord

"Look, I am standing at the door, knocking. If one of you hears me calling and opens the door, I will come in to share his meal, side by side with him" (Rv. 3:20).

Heavenly Father,
    I come to you at this time
    to call upon Your mercy and Your forgiveness.

I know that I am a sinner,
    I humbly recognize my sins,
    repenting all of them.

Forgive me, my God,
>for all that I have offended and disobeyed You,
>for the little that I have loved and honored you,
>and for the evil that I have caused my neighbor.

Forgive me, my Father,
>for the hatred that I have kept in my heart,
>for the hurts, anger and resentment,
>for the forgiveness that I have often denied,
>for the evil that I have caused,
>and for the good that I have not done.

(In the presence of the Lord, examine your conscience.)

Have pity on me!

Have mercy on me, my Father!

(Consider in your heart the possibility of seeking out those persons whom you have hurt or offended for a reconciliation. If they have passed away, ask their forgiveness in intention.)

In Your presence, my God,
>I now forgive all those who have offended me
>and caused me harm,
>And I ask forgiveness for those whom I have offended
>>and harmed.

Lord Jesus,
>I receive You in my heart
>as my only and sufficient Savior
>and I proclaim that You are my Lord.

I believe that you died for my sins
>and rose from the dead for my salvation.

I believe that you are alive,
>seated at the right hand of God the Father in power

and glory, and will come a second time
to Judge the living and the dead.

Wash me, Jesus, with Your precious Blood
and purify me from all taint of sin!

Renew my mind,
liberating me from all evil oppression
and malignant influence.

Purify my soul with Your redeeming Blood
and with the power of Your Word!

Take out of my breast this hardened heart,
marked by sin,
and give me a new heart,
similar to Yours,
full of mercy, love and forgiveness!

Fill me now with Your Holy Spirit,
so that I may understand
and live Your Word,
and obey Your laws
and Your commandments!

Save me, Lord Jesus!

Heal me, Lord Jesus!

Transform me into a true son of God!

Give me eternal life!

I firmly believe that you are producing
this salvation in my soul.

Before You,
with faith and joy,
I assume the grace of my baptism.

From now on
    I want to live in order to love and serve You
    for all the days of my life
    and to enjoy Your presence in heaven
    for all eternity.

In the power of Your name, Jesus
    and in the powerful intercession of the Virgin Mary.

Amen and amen.

Observation: If you are Catholic, seek a priest so that he may administer to you the Sacrament of Reconciliation, established by Jesus himself (cf. John 20,22-23), in order to confirm through the Sacrament the forgiveness that God grants you.

Asking for the Effusion
of the Holy Spirit

"If you then, who are evil, know how to give your children what is good, how much more will the heavenly Father give the Holy Spirit to those who ask him!" (Lk. 11:13).

Heavenly Father,
>   it is with a heart full of joy and gratitude
>   that I come to day to Your throne of grace.

I praise You and I bless you, my God
>   for Your immense love of all of us!

I thank You
>   for the marvelous salvation
>   that you have granted to mankind
>   in Jesus Christ, Your only begotten Son.

I glorify You, my God,
>   because in Him, with Him and by Him
>   we have access to all the spiritual blessings
>   and all the wealth of Your mercy!

In Jesus we have the redemption,
>   the remission of our sins.

In Him we are born again as Your children.

In Him and by Him
>   we receive all the grace necessary
>   for our sanctification.

Through Him we receive
>   from Your part,
>   the promised Holy Spirit.

My God,
>   You are my Father
>   and I beseech You in full confidence:

Baptize me now with Your Spirit!
Fill me, inundate me,
    immerse me in Your Spirit!
Lord Jesus,
    in the power of Your name, I ask:
Let Your power flow from on high,
    let flow over me now
    Your Holy Spirit,
    so that I may be full of Your power,
    as were Your apostles,
    Your disciples,
    on that day in the room of the last supper!
Come, Holy Spirit of God,
    in the name of Jesus!
I worship You,
    Holy Trinity,
    Father, Son and Holy Spirit,
    and I rejoice in You.
I believe that my supplications have been heard.
I know, my God,
    that You would never deny the Holy Spirit
    to those who ask it of You
    with faith and trust,
    for that is Your promise.
Because You are faithful and true,
    because you are zealous with Your Word
    so that it will be fulfilled,
    I now receive, through faith,
    the promised Holy Spirit.
Glory to You, my God!
Blessed are You, my Father!
In the name of Jesus.
Amen and amen.

Asking for the Gift of Perseverance in the Word of God

Today I come to You, my Father,
    and, in the name of Jesus Christ,
    I ask You to grant me the gift of perseverance
    In reading, meditating and experiencing Your Word.

Make me faithful to You, my Father,
    to Your Word
    and to Your commandments
    all the days of my life!

Father, bestow your Spirit upon me!
    That He may fill me with His power,
    wisdom, strength, perception,
    prudence, understanding,
    counsel and devotion!

Lord Jesus, You said:

> *"If you make my word your home you will indeed be my disciples, you will learn the truth and the truth shall make you free"* (Jn. 8:31b-32).

Teach me to know, love and live Your Word!

Fill me with the Holy Spirit,
    that He may activate Your Word
    in my heart,
    converting me, healing me,
    liberating me, saving me!

Grant me the grace of understanding
    that You are the very Word of God incarnate.

and by You and for You
all things were created!

In this world where we live,
so marked by sin,
where so many voices arise
proposing paths which are not Yours
words which are not Yours,
may my heart turn
more and more to You!

Touch with Your power
my understanding
about spiritual realities!

Open the ears of my soul,
so that I may hear Your voice;
the eyes of my spirit,
so that I may contemplate Your face:
and my mouth,
so that I may proclaim Your praises
and announce to my brothers and sisters
the good news of salvation!

Touch the depths of my being
so that I may love You
with all my heart,
with all my soul,
with all my spirit
and with all my might!

Blessed Holy Spirit,
come and live in me
and release Your love and power in my life,
so that I obey Your laws,
following and observing with fidelity
all the divine precepts!

Sanctify me, Lord, with Your presence
    forming the character of Jesus in me!

Shape me, Holy Spirit!

Make me once again
    in the image and likeness
    of Jesus, my Savior!
My God, I bless you,

Your Word gives me life!

Your Word saves, heals and liberates me!

Your Word gives me the understanding
    of Your will and the discernment between good and evil!

Your Word defends me from the astuteness of malevolence.

Your Word purifies and sanctifies me!

Holy Father, I ask You,
    make me always faithful and obedient to Your holy Word.

In the name of Jesus,

Amen and amen.

3

Blessings

"But if you obey
    the voice of Yahweh our God
    faithfully, keeping and
    observing all those commandments
    of his that I enjoin on you today,
    Yahweh your God will
    set you high above all the nations of the earth.

All the blessings that follow
    shall come up with you and overtake you
    if only you obey the voice of Yahweh your God.

You will be blessed
    in the town and blessed in the country.

Blessed will be the fruit of your body,
    the produce of your soil,
    the issue of your livestock,
    the increase of your cattle, the young of your flock.

Blessed will be your pannier
and your bread bin.

Blessed will you be coming in,
and blessed going out.

The enemies that rise against you Yahweh
will conquer for your sake;

They will come at you by one way
and flee before you by seven.

Yahweh will summon a blessing
for you in your barns and in
all your undertakings, and will
bless you in the land that Yahweh is giving you.

Yahweh will make of you a people
consecrated to himself as he has
sworn to you,
if you keep the commandments
of Yahweh your God and follow his ways.

All the peoples of the earth will
see that you bear the name of Yahweh
and will go in fear of you.

Yahweh will give you great store
of good things, the fruit of your body,
the fruit of your cattle
and the produce of your soil,
in the land he swore to your fathers he would give you.

Yahweh will open the heavens to you,
his rich treasure house, to give you seasonable
rain for your land and to bless all
the work of your hands.

You will make many nations your subjects,
    yet you will be subject to none.

Yahweh will put you at the head,
    not at the tail; you will
    always be on top and never
    underneath, if you obey the
    commandments of Yahweh your God
    that I enjoin on you today,
    keeping and observing them,
    not swerving to right or left from any of the works
    I enjoin on you today by following any other
    gods and serving them."

Deuteronomy 28:1-14

4

Promise

Lord Jesus, in Your presence
    I want to read, meditate,
    pray and live

I call the power of Your redemptive Blood upon me,
    purifying my mind
    and opening my heart
    to receive Your Word
    causing it to bear fruit in my life.

Send, Lord, Your Holy Spirit
    so that I may understand Your holy Word
    and have the strength of God within me to live it.

Most holy Mother, faithful Mother,
    you who always heard the Word of God
    and were able to keep it in your heart,
    pray for me and make me faithful
    to this promise which I now assume.

I, (your name)
 promise that starting today, (give the date),
 I will read, meditate, pray and live the Word of God
 all the days of my life.

I rely upon the strength and the power of the Holy Spirit
 and the powerful intercession of the Virgin Mary,
 so that I may live on this earth
 as a true son of God
 and also live eternally in His presence in heaven.

In the name of Jesus.

Amen and amen.

OTHER PUBLICATIONS

Rabboni and **Jesus Loves You** are books of prayer and meditation, based on the Word of God. They address themes that lead you to greater peace, joy, love, physical and spiritual healing, pardon, blessing, salvation, faith in Jesus, and the fullness of life.

Regis Castro

Regis Castro & Maïsa Castro

Jesus Visits You (Rachel) was written for you, woman, who loves, cares, works and suffers for your happiness and that of your family. God is now giving you the opportunity of salvation; which may never happen again like this.
Regis Castro & Maïsa Castro

Healing through Blessing
(Blessing upon Blessing)

In this book you will learn to take possession of the Word of God. You will also learn the prayer of faith that moves the hand of God.
Regis Castro & Maïsa Castro

Raïssa is a very emotional book, not only because of its subject, but for the poetry contained in its lines. The spirit of the characters is projected in such a way that it is impossible not to be touched by them.
Regis Castro

Rosary of Liberation is based on the Word of God and should be prayed with faith for the glory of the powerful name of Jesus Christ and to seek healing, salvation and liberation.
Regis Castro & Maïsa Castro

Persevere in the Love of God shows the way for this and the blessings that God pours in the lives of those who, with all confidence and loyalty, persevere in Him.
Maïsa Castro

Book of the Family – healing and salvation for you and your family presents some of the powerful weapons to be used against the spiritual forces of evil which destroy your life and that of your family.
Regis Castro & Maïsa Castro

Eternal Love presents the solution that God offers for all our problems of courtship, marriage and family.
Regis Castro & Maïsa Castro

Jesus Is My Friend was written precisely so that you may know more about the power of healing, salvation and liberation which are embodied in the name of Jesus and His Word.
Regis Castro & Maïsa Castro

Jesus Wants to Heal Your Life was inspired in talks about the Word of God given by the authors throughout their ministry of evangelization in radio programs, prayer groups, encounters, spiritual retreats, etc.
Regis Castro & Maïsa Castro

The Powerful Hand of Jesus in My Heart

The first chapter of this book may help you to open up to Jesus Christ and resolutely verify the love of God for you. The rest of the chapters also have, as their objective, the communication of a personal experience to you of the transforming power of God in your life.
Regis Castro & Maïsa Castro

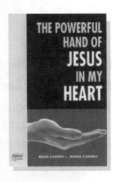

The Endearing Hands of Mary

This book is written for persons who have fallen and want to rise again, by the grace and mercy of God, through Jesus Christ and His Mother, Mary.
Regis Castro

Ping-Pong Praise

This praise, besides its principal effect which is to exalt our God, teaches everyone, from the little child to the old man, to praise Him from the heart, with simplicity and for all things, thus fulfilling His word.
Regis Castro & Maïsa Castro

God's Advice for You

The Book of Proverbs is rich in wisdom. It was necessary to divide and separate its messages into chapters that contain themes for spiritual, family, social and professional life.

Regis Castro, org.

Book of Divine Mercy, Book of Forgiveness and Book of

Joyfulness are books of prayer. They should be read slowly by you – in prayer – meditating well on the meaning of each verse and assimilating its content through faith. Thus, the Word of God, gathered into your heart, is experienced through the action of the divine Holy Spirit and will bear fruit in your life.

Regis Castro, ed.

Raïssa Castro Oliveira, ed.

Prayers of Power collects a serie of prayers, ranging from the day–to–day ones that are part of the Word of God and the tradition of the church to those spontaneously used in charismatic prayer groups.